Story of
GURU GOBIND SINGH

by
Prof. Kartar Singh

Hemkunt Press
A-78 Naraina Indl. Area, Phase-1 New Delhi-100028

© Hemkunt Press 1983
Seventh Impression 1993
ISBN 81-7010-161-1

Price Rs 60.00

Books in This Series

Printed at The Central Electric Press, A 12/1 Naraina Industrial Area, Phase-1, New Delhi 110 028

Contents

DIVINE COMMISSION

Guru Gobind Singh, the tenth and the last Guru or Prophet of the Sikhs was born to Guru Teg Bahadur and Mata Gujri on December 22nd, 1666 at Patna Sahib in Bihar. Thus, the story of his life in this world began on that day. But actually, as he tells us, his life story began much earlier. Of this he has told us in his autobiography which bears the name of Vichitra Natak which means the Wonderous Drama. In it he tells us how and for what purpose he was sent into this world by God.

He says that before he started on his earthly career, he as a bodiless spirit, was engaged in meditation in the snow-washed solitude of the seven-peaked Hemkunt mountain. 'While I was thus engaged,' adds he, 'God summoned me to His presence and addressed me thus :

"I have bestowed on you the honour of being my son and have created you for the purpose of propagating right faith and virtue among men. Go there, spread true dharma—faith and virtue sublime—and check people from committing foolish senseless acts." Thereafter He sent me into this world.

'Understand, O holy men, full well in your souls that I have taken birth for this purpose— to extend faith and virtue everywhere, to save the virtuous and the saints, and to seize and destroy root and branch, the doers of sin and evil.'

In the pages that follow we shall have an account of what he did in order to carry out his creator's orders, the 'Divine Commission' which he received when sent into this world.

BIRTH AND EARLY CHILDHOOD

Guru Gobind Singh's father, Guru Teg Bahadur, took up his duties as the ninth Sikh Guru in March 1665. Soon thereafter, he founded Sri Anandpur Sahib. The land required for the purpose was purchased by him from the ruler of the hill-state of Kahlpur.

After sometime Guru Teg Bahadur decided to make an extensive tour of the eastern parts of India. His purpose was to preach the Sikh faith among the people there. He gave the message of the brotherhood of man and the fatherhood of God, his call to humanity was to live a life of love, work, virtue, service, charity and sincere worship of God. Guru Teg Bahadur travelled by short stages. He halted at all villages, towns and cities that lay in the region through which he travelled. Everywhere he conveyed his message to the people telling them how to follow the Sikh way of life. Among the cities he visited were Agra, Allahabad, Benaras (Varanasi), Gaya and Patna. Leaving his family in Patna, he proceeded to Bengal, and then to Assam. He was in Assam at the time of his son's birth at Patna on 22nd December, 1666.

The tenth Guru's mother. Mata Gujri, named him Gobind Rai. We shall see later how he came to be called Gobind Singh.

As said above, Guru Teg Bahadur had gone on an extensive tour of the eastern parts of India. He seems to have spent about two years in Assam. Then he returned rather hurriedly to Punjab without seeing his son. This was due to Aurangzeb's policy of making Islam the one sole religion in his kingdom, the Hindus and Sikhs were passing through very hard times. The Guru could not stay away from the people when they were suffering. He felt that his place was with them. So he returned to Punjab, leaving his family at Patna.

A little over five years of the tenth Guru's life were spent in the city of his birth. His early schooling, therefore was done at Patna. His maternal uncle, Sri Kirpal, taught him Gurmukhi and the Sikh scriptures. He also studied the Bihari language at Patna.

Sri Kirpal also trained him in the arts of archery and swordsmanship. He soon became a great marksman. His arrows never missed the target. His skill in the use of the sword was equally great and marvellous.

6

During these early years, he gave clear signs of the sort of the life which he was to lead later. He was active and full of mirth. He loved to play the soldier and to be a leader. He had an army of playmates around. They all looked upon him as their leader. Usually, he would divide them into two equal groups. He placed himself at the head of one of the groups. The other group had a captain of their own choice. He made the two groups engage in games and matches requiring skill, courage, strength and patience.

He was so fond of playing with his playmates, that as a rule he returned home quite late in the evening. This delayed the recitation of RAHIRAS, the evening prayer. By custom, the RAHIRAS in the Patna Sahib Gurdwara is still read after the usual hour prescribed for it.

He was bold and fearless. One day, he was playing with his friends in one of the main streets of the city. The Chief Officer or Nawab of Patna came that way, accompanied by his bodyguard and a number of officers. The Nawab's servants called upon the boys to salute the Nawab. Hearing this, the child-guru Sri Gobind Rai, said to his comrades, "No, brothers, we are not going to salute or say *salam* to this man. This he did as a protest because Aurangzeb's policy of oppression against Hindus and Sikhs.

7

LIFE AT PATNA

Gobind Rai, as Guru Gobind Singh was then called, was a charming child. His conduct and behaviour won him a large number of devotees and admirers. He came to be loved by many—both young and old, rich and poor, learned and simple, Hindus and Muslims. Among his Hindu admirers was a learned Brahmin named Shivdutt, who looked upon him as God-in-Man. Raja Fateh Chand Maini and his wife were even more devoted than Pandit Shivdutt. They had been conquered in a singular way. They had no son. They were very sad on that account. They urged Pandit Shivdutt to pray for them. He said to them, "The God Himself is in this very city in human form. Pray sincerely for what you desire. He will come to you. He will fulfil your desire."

They did as desired. They would every day for hours sit praying and longing for Him to come and bless them. One day, as they were sitting in prayer, two little arms were flung round the queen's neck in a light embrace of love. Then a sweet charming voice spoke into her ear, "Mother, I have come."

The king and the queen were glad and very happy beyond measure. The Divine Child or God-in-Man had come to their house and called himself their son. Their long-cherished wish for a son had been fulfilled. They now had a son, what a grand glorious son !

When Gobind Rai left Patna for Anandpur the Raja and Rani converted their palace into a *dharmsala,* a place of worship and charity. The gifts which they had got from the child a set of arms and dress, were placed by them in a place of honour in the house. They lived lives of peace and bliss.

Several years later, they went to Anandpur to see their beloved child. By then he was a full-grown man of three and twenty and the tenth Guru. He came out to receive them and treated them as their own son would have done. After some time they returned home with a copy of the Sacred Book as his gift. They installed it in the same room where they had earlier placed the arms and the dress. They lived happily for a long time. After they left the world, the people kept the memory alive by making their home a temple which exists to this day. Thus did Guru Gobind Singh prove a true son to this pair, helping them to a peaceful life in this world as well as in the next.

There was hardly a home in Patna which did not have a member who was Gobind Rai's admirer. Among his Muslim admirers were two brothers named

Nawab Karim Bakhsh and Nawab Rahim Bakhsh. They made an offering of a village and two gardens to the charming child. These are still attached to the Gurdwara at Patna.

Another Muslim admirer of his at that time was Pir Bhikhan Shah. He was a prominent Saint. He lived at the village named Thaska in the district of Karnal, now in Haryana. On the day that Guru Gobind Singh was born, the Pir did something unusual for a Muslim. He looked towards the east, in the direction of Patna. Then he made a deep and respectful bow. This act was not only unusual for a Muslim, but also forbidden. As we know, Muslims in this country bow to the west, in the direction of Mecca. His disciples felt surprised. They asked him why he had bowed to the east. The Pir replied, 'Far away in the east is a city named Patna. In that city a holy Saint has been born. He is to perform wonders. He will destroy the evil and wicked people. He will fight against sin, evil, and false religion. He will champion

the cause of virtue and true religion. I am bowing the God's representation in human form. I shall soon be going to that sacred city in order to get a sight of him. The sight will be a feast for my eyes and a blessing for my soul.'

True to his resolve, the Pir soon set out for Patna. He had some disciples and servants with him. In due course, he reached his destination. He went straight to the house where Gobind Rai then lived. He bowed and sat near the door. He was asked what he wanted, why he sat there in that way. He replied, 'I have come from a far-off place. My object is to have a look at the holy child born and living in this blessed house. He is a massenger of God.

Mata Gujri was informed of the fakir at her door. She was told what he wanted. At first she hesitated a bit. She made some excuses to send him off. But the Pir was firm. He said, 'I have travelled hundreds of miles in order to have a look at the holy child. I will not move from this place until my wish is granted. I will neither eat nor drink anything till then. His wish had to be granted at last. As soon as he saw the child, he made a deep and respect - ful bow and touched his tiny little feet. He had purposely brought with him two earthen pots.

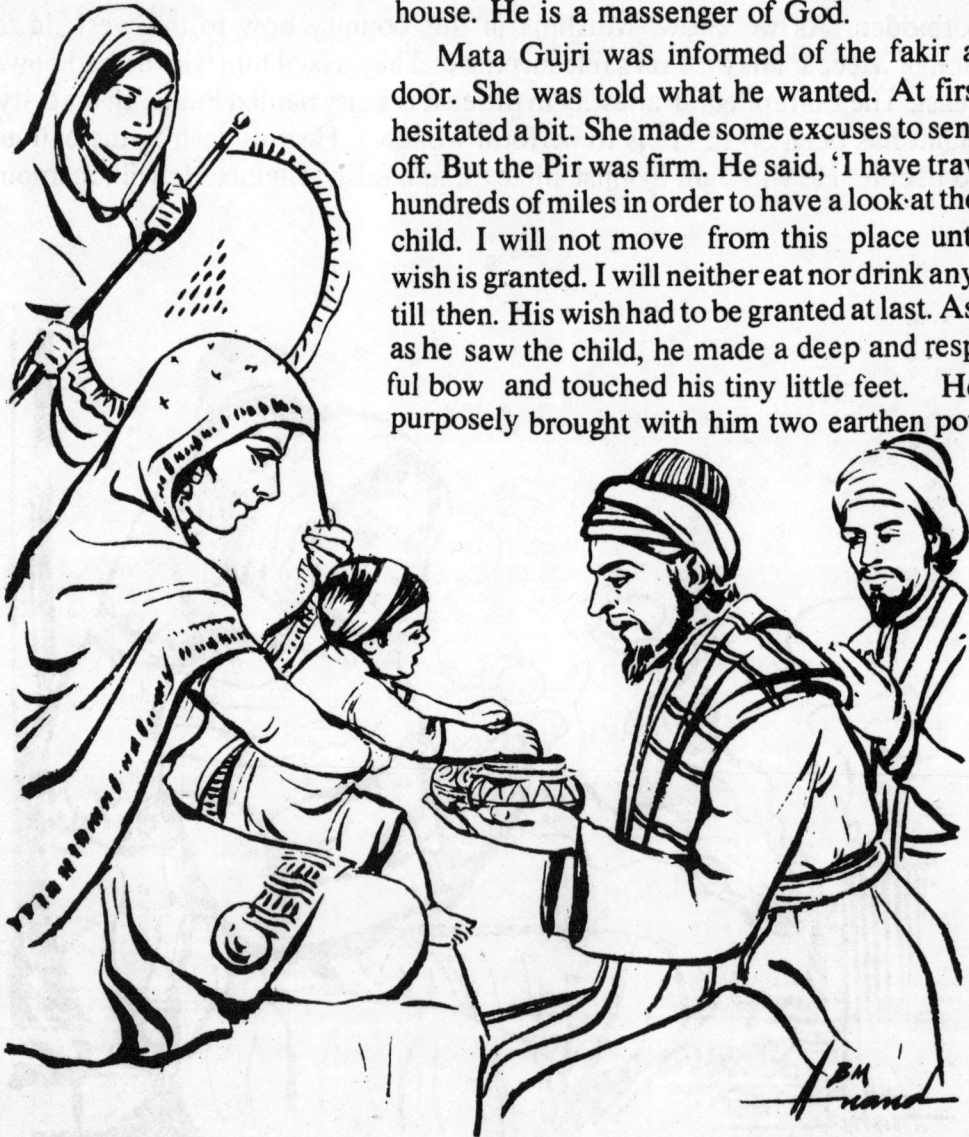

They contained sweetmeat. One of them had been brought from the shop of a Hindu confectioner. The other had been brought from a Muslim confectioner's shop. The Pir softly held the two pots before the holy child. Having done this, he sat with hands folded and eyes fixed on the child. The latter covered one of the pots with his right hand. He covered the other with his left hand. Then he smiled and looked at the Pir. He seemed to say. 'Are you satisfied?' The Pir, thereupon, made a deeper and longer bow. There was a look of complete satisfaction and gratitude on his face.

The Pir's disciples who had come with him said to him, 'we are unable to understand all this. Kindly explain it to us.

The Pir replied 'I wanted to know whether this man of God will favour the Hindus or the Muslims. I said to myself, "If he is to favour the Hindus, he will put his hand on the pot from the Hindu shop. If he is to favour the Muslims, he will put his hand on the pot got from the Muslim shop." He has read my thoughts. He has covered both the pots. He means to assure me that Hindus and Muslims will be equally dear to him. He will help the Hindus, if they need his help. He will help the Muslims if they need his help. This has gladdened me immensely.'

The Pir then returned to his home in Punjab. He remained an ardent admirer of Guru Gobind Singh all through his life.

11

HIS FIRST GREAT SACRIFICE

As desired by Guru Tegh Bahadur, his family started towards Punjab in February 1672. In about six months, that is in August of that year, the party reached Lakhnaur in the district of Ambala. The rains had begun. The rivulets, which crossed the path to Anandpur, were all flooded and difficult to cross. Hence the party had to halt at Ambala to let the rivulets subside. The party spent about five months at Lakhnaur, resumed its journey in January 1673, and reached Anandpur in due course.

At Anandpur, Sri Gobind Rai was now passing the happiest days of his life. His regular education was begun now. He had already learnt Sanskrit and Persian as well as the Sikh scripture. Special and suitable arrangements were made for training him in horsemanship and the use of arms. The time which he could snatch from his studies and training exercises, he spent in games and recreation.

His blissful life at Anandpur was soon cut short rather abruptly. One day, as he came home after a spell of play, he found a group of strangers sitting before his father. They were all sad and down-cast. His father, too, was sad and lost in thought. He asked his father why he was so sad and lost in thought. Then, turning to the group of people sitting there he said, 'Who are these people? They seem to be lost in sadness and despair. What have they come for? What have they been telling you? What are you thinking about, dear father?'

The Guru replied, 'They are Pundits from Kashmir. They are face to face with a life-and-death problem. Their Muslim Governor has told them to choose between Islam and death. They are told either to become Muslims or be prepared to die. They want neither this nor that. They have come to me for advice. It is a very serious problem. Our Muslim rulers are making life miserable. They are treating their Hindu subjects with utmost injustice and cruelty. They have no compassion. They have ceased to be human. They have come to behave like wild, fierce beasts. Their forzen, stony hearts need to be melted and softened. Their inhuman behaviour has to be made human. There seems to be but one way to do all this. Some great holy man should sacrifice himself. How and where to find such a one, is the question before me. That is the problem which has made me sad and lost in deep, serious thought. May God guide and help me.'

Sri Gobind Rai was hardly eight years of age. He at once said to his father, 'For that great sacrifice, dear father, who can be fitter and worthier than you.' The Guru

12

accepted his son's suggestion. He said to the Pundits, 'Go and say to the Governor, "Guru Tegh Bahadur is our guide and leader. First make him a Muslim, we will follow his example.' I am sure he will agree. Leave the rest to me. I shall act as the Lord above directs me to do.'

The Pundits made no delay in acting as advised by the Guru. As a result, he was arrested in July 1675. He was fettered, and shut up in an iron cage. He was taken to Delhi. There he was publicly beheaded in the Chandni Chowk on November 11, 1675. The place where the Guru was beheaded is called Sis Ganj. A gurdwara was built there by Sardar Baghel Singh in 1790.

13

In this way did Guru Tegh Bahadur make the supreme sacrifice for the sake of protecting the Hindu religion.

He wanted to inspire the people with the spirit to stand up boldly for human rights, including that of religious beliefs and worship. He wanted to make them be ever up and doing for the sake of righteousness, be prepared to suffer and make sacrifices in the cause of freeing the land from the yoke of oppressors, and be ever prepared to suffer in order to relieve others of their troubles. 'Fear none and strike fear in none' was the theme of his teaching.

THE GURU'S GREAT RESOLVE

After Guru Tegh Bahadur's execution, his head and body were left exposed in the street in order to serve as a lesson to those who would think of going against the Emperor's will and the rules of Islam. Strong guards were placed to prevent their removal. The Guru's execution had a staggering effect on the Sikhs. Nobody from the 'high-caste' Sikhs came forward to claim the martyred Guru's body for the purpse of cremation. Only a 'low-caste' Lubana Sikh, named Lakhi Shah, had the courage to secretly take away the headless body in a cart to his hut outside the city. He erected a pyre within his hut, placed the body on it, and set fire to his hut in order to make out that it was all an accident. His hut was in the village of Rakab Ganj, near Delhi. The site is now marked by a gurdwara named Rakab Ganj. It was erected by Sardar Baghel Singh in 1790.

Another 'low-caste' Ranghreta Sikh, named Jaita, belonging to the sweeper class, took up the Guru's head and hurried away with it to Anandpur. There he presented it to the martyred Guru's son. Guru Gobind Singh, who was then a mere child of less than nine, was deeply touched with the dauntless courage and extreme devotion of the Ranghreta Sikh. Flinging his arms round Bhai Jaita's neck, he declared, *'Ranghrete Guru ke bete*—Ranghretas are the Guru's own sons. Here through you, I embrace them all as such.'

Guru Gobind Singh cremated the head with due Sikh rites. A Gurdwara called Sis Ganj at Anandpur, marks the site.

Guru Gobind Singh was deeply grieved to learn that the execution of Guru Tegh Bahadur had so thoroughly staggered and demoralized the Sikhs that nobody from the high class Sikhs came forward to claim the martyred Guru's body. Only a Ranghreta Sikh had the daring to pick up the head, and a Lubana Sikh took the risk of taking away and cremating the headless body. Nobody from the high class Sikhs had shown the courage of his convictions and openly declare that they were the martyred Guru's Sikhs. On the contrary, when questioned by the officials whether they were Sikhs, they had all, except the Guru's immediate followers, denied their religion.

The Guru saw in this the danger of backsliding among the Sikhs. 'It is possible' thought he, 'that the Sikhs might fall back into the great sea from which they have been taken out.' Hence he vowed that he would make it impossible for the Sikhs to hide their creed in future. He would give them such form and appearance, some such

15

distinguishing marks, that even a single Sikh mixed up with thousands of others would be recognizable at once, most easily and unmistakably. A distinctive form and appearance would serve another purpose, too. The Sikhs would have to be true and pure in order to maintain the dignity of their distinctive guise, so that none might have a chance or justification to remark, 'Fie upon you ! You are a Sikh of Guru

Nanak—Gobind Singh, and you are behaving in such an un-Sikh-like manner.' In this way the Sikhs would stand out distinct from others not only in external appearance, but also in internal virtue and day-to day life.

SAYYID BUDHU SHAH

Raja Medni Parkash, chief of the Himalayan hill-state of Nahan, invited Guru Gobind Singh to his state. The Guru accepted the invitation. He reached Nahan on April 14, 1685 and founded there a fort which he named Paonta. There, sitting on the beautiful banks of the Jamuna, he thought of what should be done to free his countrymen from the bonds of sin, suffering, and slavery. He applied himself closely to self-education. As a child he had, during his stay at Patna, learnt to speak Bihari. He had learnt Gurmukhi from his mother and maternal uncle. As he tells us in his autobiography called *Vichitra Natak*, 'his father had given him instruction of various kinds'. He had learnt Persian from a Muslim teacher. Now at Patna he went through the whole range of epic literature in Sanskrit. At the same time, he mastered the art of composing poetry in Hindi and Punjabi. In Hindi he developed a style which has remained unsurpassed. He translated the old stories of Indian heroes, as found in the Purans, the Ramayan, and the Mahabharat. He engaged fifty two poets to help him in this heavy task. The keynote of this vast literature in optimism, freedom from superstition and strong faith in the oneness of God and of all humanity—the fatherhood of God and the brotherhood of man.

His purpose in creating this literature was to infuse a new spirit among his followers, and steel their hearts against all injustice and tyranny. The tyranny that then prevailed was not only political but also religious and social. It was being practised everyday in kitchens, at village wells, in temples and hundreds of other places visited by the people. It was far worse than any other sin or crime. Guru Gobind Singh says :

'The sins committed in the name of religion are such as put even greatest sins to blush.'

In order to fit himself for the struggle, he practised every form of manly exercise, such as riding, hunting, archery, and sword play. At Sadhaura, about twenty five kilometers from Paonta, there lived a Sayyid Faqir named Pir Budhu Shah. He learnt that Guru Gobind Singh was staying so near him. He went to see him. The Guru received him warmly. The Sayyid said, 'People think me to be a pious man of religion. But I know that I am a sinner. I am terribly afraid of what may happen to me after death. Get me pardoned for my sins. Save me from God's wrath. Tell me how to win His praise and become acceptable to him.'

The Guru replied, 'God is all mercy and forgiveness. He loves us all as a good father loves his children. Repent your mistakes and sins from the bottom of your heart. Resolve never to do wrong again. Keep busy in doing good deeds. Help all that need your help. All the time be humble and truthful. Avoid pride and vanity. Always feel God to be watching all your actions. Feel Him to be knowing all your feelings, desires and thoughts. Think, feel, or desire nothing that may displease Him. Ever remember Him, and pray to Him for light, grace and mercy. If you live such a life, you need have no fears about your life after death.

Sayyid Budhu Shah was delighted to hear these words. He bowed and promised to live and act as advised by the Guru. After some time he returned to his home in Sadhaura.

18

BATTLE OF BHANGANI

A few days after Sayyid Budhu Shah's return home, five hundred Pathans in military uniform came to him. They said to him, 'Our profession is military service. We were employed in the army of Emperor Aurangzeb. We have been dismissed for a minor fault. Now no one is prepared to employ us. All are afraid of the mighty Mughal. We have come to you for help. Get us employed somewhere. We shall be faithful to our employer and greatful to you. We shall not bring a bad name to you in any way.

Sayyid Budhu Shah decided to help them. He knew that Guru Gobind Singh had employed a large number of Muslims in his army. He decided to request him to enlist the Pathans also in his army. He took them to the Guru. He told him their story and their need. He recommended them for enlistment in the Guru's army. The Guru agreed. He took them into his service and gave them handsome salaries. He fixed a salary of five rupees a day for each officer and one rupee a day for each soldier. The five officers' names were : Haiyat Khan, Kale Khan, Nijabat Khan, Umre Khan and Bhikhan Khan.

The Pathans were with the Guru at Paonta, along with his main army. There he was suddenly attacked by the hill-chiefs. They were led by Raja Bhim Chand of Bilaspur.

The above said Pathans heard that the hill-chiefs were about to attack the Guru. Four of the five Pathan officers, with the four hundered soldiers under them decided to desert the Guru. They went over to and joined his enemies. One Pathan officer, Kale Khan, and the soldiers under him, however remained faithful to the Guru.

The Guru lost no time in informing Sayyid Budhu Shah of the said Pathan soldiers' misconduct. The Sayyid felt this misbehaviour to be a personal disgrace to himself. He made up his mind to make amends, to remove the disgrace. He decided to help the Guru. Accordingly, he joined the Guru along with his two brothers, his four sons, and his seven hundred disciples.

Five hundred Udasi *sadhus*, who had been fattening themselves on the rich food served in the Guru's kitchen, were deeply dismayed on hearing the news of the coming battle. They feared that the Guru might ask them to take the field. They did not want to run any such risk. So they ran away during the night. Their leader,

Mahant Kirpal, was the only Udasi who did not go.

Next morning the Guru was informed of what had happened. The Guru smiled and said, 'The root, at any rate, is left. As the root still exists, the tree shall grow and bear flowers and fruits. If the Mahant had also gone, the Udasis would have been altogether uprooted and finished. They would have been expelled from Sikhism.'

The Guru had stationed his troops on an eminence about twelve kilometers north of Paonta and near the village Bhangani. A severe and bloody battle was fought there. Sayyid Budhu Shah, his brothers, his sons, and his disciples all fought with great bravery and devotion. They shouted like thunder. They killed a large number of the Guru's enemies. They drove the enemy before them as a hurricane drives dry leaves and straw. Two of the Sayyied's sons and several disciples fell fighting for the Guru. The Guru's enemies suffered heavy losses and a crushing defeat.

Mahant Kirpal also fought with bravery. He challenged Haiyat Khan, one of the four Pathan officers who had deserted the Guru, and killed him with his wooden club. When the Pathans had run away, the Guru congratulated the Mahant and said, 'Well done, my saint soldier, well done, indeed.'

The Battle of Bhangani was fought on April 16, 1689. After the battle, Sayyid Budhu Shah went to the Guru to take leave of him. His surviving sons and disciples were with him. The Guru said to him, 'You have proved to be a true lover and worshipper of God. Deem not your sons as dead. They shall live for ever in God's presence. Only those really die who care not for God and their duty, who turn cowards on the field of battle.'

Sayyid Budhu Shah, thereupon, said, 'O true Guru, I do not at all mourn for my sons who have died fighting for you. They have laid down their lives in a good and noble cause. They have gone to enjoy lasting bliss in Paradise. I am proud of them.'

The Guru considered how best to reward the Sayyid. He conferred on him the most precious gift of God's name. He told him how to attain union with Him. He made him other gifts as well. He was, at that time, combing his hair. A Sikh was standing near, holding the Guru's turban. The Sayyid requested the Guru to give him the comb with his loose hair in it. The Guru laid the comb with his loose hair in it upon his turban held by the Sikh. He presented the turban and the comb to Sayyid Budhu Shah. He said, 'Keep these in memory of this day.' He also gave him a robe of honour, a *kirpan* or sword, a turban, and a *Hukamnama*—an order to his Sikhs to treat the Sayyid and his descendants with deep respect and kindness. The Guru's comb, hair, and *kirpan* were later acquired from his descendants by Raja Bharpur

21

Singh of Nabha and preserved as sacred relics in that Sikh state.

Sayyid Budhu Shah returned home. His wife and other relatives began to mourn for his two sons who had fallen on the battle-field. He advised them not to mourn but to rejoice. His sons, he said, had not died. They had gone to Paradise to live there in joy and peace for ever. His wife dried her tears. She blessed her sons. She became a disciple of the Guru like her husband. Long afterwards, she and her husband were killed by agents of Aurangzeb. Their only fault was that they had faith in Guru Gobind Singh, they had become his disciples. Both of them died fighting like true soldier-disciples.

The Guru stayed at Bhangani for a few days, in order to dispose of the dead and take care of the wounded. Then he decided to return to Anandpur. From

Bhangani he went back to Paonta. From Paonta he went to Sadhaura to meet and bless Sayyid Budhu Shah and his wife. He returned to Anandpur after an absence of four years.

In order to ensure the safety of the city against attacks, he strengthened its fortifications. He constructed five forts which were named Anandgarh, Lohgarh, Fategarh, Kesgarh and Holgarh.

BATTLES OF NADAUN AND GULER

We have seen how the hill chiefs, led by Raja Bhim Chand, had tasted the Guru's steel and suffered crushing defeat at Bhangani. After that bitter experience he decided to make friends with the Guru. He sent a messenger to the Guru's darbar for the purpose of sounding him. The Guru told the messenger that all aggression in the past had been on the Raja's side. If he really desired peace, he need have no fears on account of the Guru. Thereupon Raja Bhim Chand came, asked forgiveness for the past, and prayed for being regarded as a humble friend and ally. The Guru readily agreed, and ensured him of his friendship and help if he behaved well.

About a year passed in peace. But the peace was then broken and the Guru had to engage once again in warfare.

The hill-chiefs had not paid the tribute to the Emperor of Delhi for a number of years. In 1690, Main Khan, Governor of Jammu, sent Alif Khan, a military commander, to make the demand and collect the arrears of the tribute. He reached Nadaun and from there sent word to Bhim Chand and others that they should either pay the tribute due from them or get ready for battle. They decided to seek the Guru's advice and aid. He advised them to resist the demand, for if they yielded now, more and more would be demanded in the years to come. He agreed to take part in the struggle. A battle was fought at Nadaun which ended in the success of the allies.

Some time thereafter a general named Hussain Khan or Hussaini was sent to collect the tribute and to finish the Guru.

Raja Ajmer Chand, who had succeeded Raja Bhim Chand, and many other hill-chiefs joined the invader. They paid the tribute and proceeded with him towards Anandpur. But before falling upon that city, they decided to kill Raja Gopal of Guler, who had not yielded. He sought the Guru's help. The latter sent a strong force of his choicest warriors under the command of Bhai Sangatia Singh. A bloddy battle was faught. Hussain, his two military officers, Raja Kirpal Chand of Katoch and many prominent officers of the hill-chief's army were slain. A large part of their army was also killed. The rest fled in terror. Ajmer Chand saved his life by taking to his heels. Bhai Sangatia Singh and seven of his companions were also slain.

The Guru had been only a helper in the battles of Nadaun and Guler. But the victories at both places were considered to be his. The success of Guru Gobind Singh had caused a good deal of anxiety to the Emperor. In consequence, he had, in

November 1693 issued orders to his Faujdars that the Guru should be warned not to assemble his Sikhs. This does not seem to have produced much effect. It was soon reported to the Emperor that the Sikhs had caused a good deal of disturbance round Lahore and a general order for massacre was issued. The Emperor himself was too busy in the Deccan. Therefore, he sent his son, Prince Muazzim, afterwards known as Bahadur Shah, to set right the affairs in Punjab. The Prince took up his position in Lahore. He sent Mirza Beg with a strong force to punish

the Guru and the Rajas. The Rajas were severely punished but the Guru was left alone through the intercession of Bhai Nand Lal, who was a devout Sikh and a secretary of the Prince.

Bhai Nand Lal seems to have brought about some kind of understanding between the Government and the Guru. On hearing from Bhai Nand Lal about the spiritual greatness of the Guru, the Prince became a friend and admirer of Guru Gobind Singh. He arranged matters in such a way that, for the time being at least, the Guru made up his quarrel with the Mughal Government. He advised his followers to render to the Government what was due to it. This is clear from the following significant statement recorded in the *Vichitra Natak* :—

> 'The house of (Baba) Nanak and that of Babar
> Both derive their authority from God Himself.
> Recognise the former as supreme in religion
> And the latter as supreme in secular affairs.'

THE GURU'S AMAZING CALL

The Beloved Five

Guru Nanak had worked to create a casteless society, a society in which no one was considered high or low simply on account of having been born in this or that caste. His successors had worked on the same lines. Hosts of low-caste people were taken into the fold of Sikhism, made members of the *Brotherhood of Man* founded by the Guru. The result was that jats, who were considered *Sudras*, enjoyed the greatest privilege along with the *Khatris*, and the *Brahmins* were no longer held in esteem.

But much was still left to be done before a really casteless society could be fully and securely established. Guru Gobind Singh decided to cut at the root of all such customs and practices as stood in the way of a complete unification of the nation. He wanted to create a united and strong body of men who would be pure enough to free themselves from the oppression of priests and rulers, and, at the same time, be strong enough to maintain this freedom.

Guru Nanak as well as all his successor Gurus used to let their hair and beards grow their natural length. On their heads they wore turbans and not caps. Most Sikhs followed their Guru's example. They had long hair and flowing beards. They wore turbans on their heads. But quite a considerable minority continued to shave even after embracing Sikhism.

Guru Gobind Singh, as said already, wanted to give the Sikhs a distinct appearance, a distinct uniform, so that a Sikh mixed even with a thousand non-Sikhs be easily and immediately recognizable.

Thinking thus, the Guru sent out orders that all Sikhs should let their hair and beards grow their natural length, that they should wear turbans and not caps.

In the beginning of the year 1699 A.D., the Guru sent out special invitations to all Sikhs. They were desired to attend a special gathering which was to be held on the occasion of that year's Baisakhi day. There was a good response. As the Baisakhi day approached, a number of Sikhs began to arrive at Anandpur.

The Guru ordered that carpets be spread on a raised piece on the open space near Sri Kesgarh. A beautiful tent was also set up nearby.

On the day just before the Baisakhi day, which fell on March 30, 1699, a big open air meeting was held at the above-said place. As soon as the morning prayers

27

were over, the Guru went into the tent. He remained there for some time. The assembled Sikhs wondered what their Guru was doing inside the tent. He came out at last. His appearance was altogether different from what it had usually been. His eyes were shining like fire. His face was hardset and red. His naked sword shone in his uplifted hand. He looked like a warrior about to jump into a battle-field. In a voice as of thunder he said, 'My dear Sikhs, my beloved sons, this sword of mine wants to taste the blood of a Sikh. Is there any among you ready to offer his neck for the purpose, to lay down his life at a call from me?"

All present grew pale on hearing such a strange demand. There was no response to this amazing, breath-taking call. The Guru repeated it. Still there was no reply. A third time he spoke in a louder, more thundering voice. 'Is there any true Sikh of mine among you? If so, let he come up and give me his head as an offering, as a proof of his faith in me.' After some minutes, Bhai Daya Ram, a Khatri of Lahore, stood up and said, 'O true King, my head is at your service. Cut it off from the trunk, make it fall at your sacred feet.'

The Guru took him by the arm. He dragged him into the tent. The assembled Sikhs soon heard from inside the tent the sound of a sword-blow. They then heard the sound of a body falling on the ground. They saw a stream of blood coming out of the tent. It meant that the Guru had beheaded Bhai Daya Ram.

After a while the Guru came out of the tent. His face was redder than before. His eyes were red as blood. The sword in his uplifted hand was dripping with fresh blood. In a loud thundering voice he called out, 'Is there any Sikh ready to give me his head?' The Sikhs gathered there felt convinced that the Guru really meant what he said. They were convinced that Bhai Daya Ram had been killed. There was dead silence. The Guru called again, there was no response. He called for the third time.

On the third call, Bhai Dharam Das, a jat Sikh of Delhi, stood up and said, 'O true king, take my head. Death with your sword will give me new life, happy and ever lasting.'

The Guru caught him by the arm. He dragged him forcefully into the tent The same two sounds of a sword-blow, and that of a body falling on the ground were heard. As before, a stream of fresh-drawn blood came out from the tent. The Sikhs gathered there were convinced that Bhai Dharam Das, too, had been killed. They were filled with terror. Many of them fled for their lives.

After a short time, the Guru came out again. He looked fiercer than before. His face and eyes were redder. Waving his sword above his head, he called out, 'Is there any other Sikh ready to offer me his head? I am in great need of the heads of my dear Sikhs. Be quick.'

More and more Sikhs slipped away. The gathering grew thinner and thinner. Every face was pale. All lips were dry. All heads were lowered. All eyes were downcast. Some went to the Guru's mother, Mata Gujri. They complained to her against the Guru. 'He seems to have gone mad,' said they. 'He is killing his Sikhs. Remove him from guruship. Let a grandson of yours take his place as the Guru.'

Thereupon, she sent a messenger to him in order to call him into her presence. But he was in no mood to receive, heed, or listen to anyone. He repeated the call for another head. On the third such call Bhai Mohkam Chand, a washerman of Dwarka, stood up and offered his head. The Guru treated him in the same manner in which he had treated the other two. A stream of blood was seen coming out from the tent. 'So another Sikh has been killed,' thought the Sikhs gathered outside the tent.

After a short time the Guru came out again. In the same manner as before, he called for another head. Again there was no response. Some more Sikhs ran away. Others sat with lower heads and fastbeating hearts. The Guru repeated the call. On the third call, Bhai Sahib Chand, a barbar of Bidar, stood up and begged the Guru to

29

accept his head. The Guru treated him in the manner as he had treated the other three. 'So the fouth Sikh has been killed,' thought the Sikhs gathered there.

After a while, the Guru again came out of the tent. He was, as before, waving his sword covered with fresh blood. He again called for another head. At this a large number of the Sikhs ran away. For a while there was no response to the Guru's call. It was repeated twice. Then Bhai Himmat Rai, a water-carrier of Jagannath, stood up and offered his head. The Guru treated him in the same way in which he had treated the other four. 'So the fifth Sikh has been killed.' thought the Sikhs gathered outside the tent.

This time the Guru stayed a bit longer inside the tent. At last he came out. He was dressed in bright saffron-coloured garments. His sword was sheathed and hung by his side. His face was beaming with joy and satisfaction. He was followed by five Sikhs dressed exactly like him. Who were they ? Oh wonder ! They were the same who had given their heads to the Guru. They had been killed. Had they been brought back to life ? Their faces, their dress, and their whole appearance were all like the Guru's.

The Guru seated them near himself. Then he rose and said aloud, 'When Baba Nanak tested his Sikhs, only one Sikh, Baba Laihna, stood the test successfuly. Now I, on the other hand, have found five Sikhs totally devoted to the Guru. I am immensely pleased. It is a matter of joy for all of us. The Sikh faith will grow and flourish well and ever. These five are my *Panj Piare,* my beloved five. They are in my form, I am in theirs. They are one with me. I am in them. They are in me.'

BIRTH OF THE KHALSA

After addressing the gathering in the manner given above, the Guru added, 'I am going to do something today which will make this day most memorable in our history, something which will mark a turning point in the history of my people and the country.

'So far, the custom of *charnpahul* has been in vogue for admitting persons to the Sikh faith. According to this custom a vessel of water was placed before the Guru. He touched the water with his toe. The person who wanted to become a Sikh drank a little of this water. Such has been the practice so far. It developed humility. That virtue is very precious and essential. As Baba Nanak has said, "Sweetness and humility are the essence of all good qualities." But the times have changed. Sweetness and humility alone cannot successfully meet the challenge of the greatly changed and rapidly changing times. Now we need fearless bravery, dauntless courage, and great skill in the use of arms. We need them for the defence and maintenance of the Sikh faith and the Sikh nation. We need them to free our country from the crushing rule of cruel foreigners. We need them in order to bring to the common man the blessings of love, justice, equality, and brotherliness.

'From today the Sikh nation shall be called the *Khalsa. Charnpahul* will give place to *Khande da Amrit* the nectar of two edged sword. The person desiring to become a Sikh, to become a member of the Khalsa Brotherhood, will drink water that has been stirred with a Khanda or two-edged sword. This water shall be called *amrit* (nectar). I shall presently let you see how *amrit* is to be administered.

Those who partake of this *amrit* will be changed from jackals to lions, from sparrows to hawks. They will be called *Singhs* or Lions. All castes, all people, are equally welcome to take the *amrit.* I mean to make all Sikhs give up and forget for ever their previous castes. I want to combine them all into one Brotherhood, the Khalsa. In that Brotherhood, all will be equal in all respects, the lowest with the highest.'

The Guru then took fresh clean water in a vessel of steel. He knelt beside it in the soldierly fashion. He told the Five Beloved to stand before him in a semi-circle. They were told to fix their eyes on the Guru and fix their minds on God. He then began to stir the water in the steel vessel with a *khanda* or two-edged sword. At the same time he went on reciting the sacred verses of Gurbani which he had fixed for the ceremony. Then he said, 'In this vessel of steel I have prepared the *amrit* or the

31

baptismal nectar. With it I shall baptize the Five Dear Ones. Then I shall baptize others. But before proceeding to do that, I shall show you what wonderful power the *amrit* possesses.'

Saying this, he put some of it aside for birds to drink. Upon this, two sparrows came there. They sipped some of the nectar. Immediately they flew away to a short distance. There they began to fight fiercely. They fought like two kings fighting for a kingdom. Each was bent upon killing the other. They continued fighting till both were dead.

Thereupon the Guru said to his Sikhs, 'You have seen what wounderful power the *amrit* possesses. All who take it will acquire the same spirit as did the sparrows here. They will become fearless, brave, and warlike.'

A Sikh went to the Guru's wife, Mata Jitoji. He informed her of the *amrit* which the Guru had prepared. He gave her an account of the incident of the two sparrows. Hearing this, she said to herself, 'Let me go and sweeten the *amrit*. It will have a sweetening effect on those who take it.' She took some Indian sweetmeat called *patashas* made from white sugar. She took them to the Guru. Reaching there, she stood waiting before him. Soon he raised his eyes. He saw her with the sweets in her hands. He said to her, 'You have come at a very appropriate time. You have brought something which will prove very useful. I am going to change my Sikhs to Singhs or Lions. The *amrit* prepared by me will produce fearless courage, moral and physical strength and bravery. These qualities are very useful. They are very much in need in these days. They will be needed still more urgently in the times to come. But they alone can prove dangerous and harmful. They must be accompanied by sweetness of temper and peace-loving nature. The sweet brought by you will have that effect. Pour them in the *amrit* here. Those who will take it will be brave, strong, and fearless like lions. At the same time, they will possess the grace of womanly sweetness.

Mata Jitoji poured the *patashas* into the *amrit* which the Guru had prepared. He dissolved them in it by stirring it with two-edged sword. Then he stood up, holding the vessel of *amrit* in his hands. He made the Beloved Five kneel on their left knees in the soldierly fashion. He told them to fix their eyes on his. He gazed into the eyes of each of them, turn by turn. At the same time, he threw, five times, showers of the *amrit* in the Dear One's face. Each time he called upon the Dear One to say aloud. *Wahiguru ji ka khalsa, Sri Wahiguru ji ki fateh*. Then the Guru sprinkled the nectar five times on the dear one's hair and eyes. Then he said to one of them, 'Hold the steel vessel in both hands. Drink some of it. Then pass the vessel on to the next Dear one. Let the vessel go round, forward and backward in this way, till the whole of the nectar has been drunk up.'

32

As we have seen, the Beloved Five belonged to different castes. One of them belonged to a so-called high caste. He was a *Khatri.* The other four were the so-called low-castes—a Jat, a washerman or calico-printer, a water-carrier and a barber. For such persons to drink from the same vessel was an act not heard of ever or any where before in India. It was a revolutionary act. It shocked all who were proud of their high castes.

Then the Guru said, 'Those who take the amrit become my lions. I name them Singhs. Therefore, the names of my Five Dear Ones will no longer be Daya Ram, Dharam Das, Mukham Chand, Sahib Chand, and Himmat Rai. Their names will henceforth be Daya Singh, Dharam Singh, Mukham Singh, Sahib Singh and Himmat Singh. From now on the names of my Sikhs will not end in 'Ram,' 'Das,' 'Rai' 'Mal', 'Chand' etc. They will all end in Singh. My Sikhs must always wear the following five articles whose Punjabi names begin with 'K' sound, namely, *Kes*(uncut hair) *Kangha* (comb), *Kirpan* (sword), *Kachha* (short drawers), and *Kara* (steel bracelet). My Sikhs should carry arms. They should be ever able and ready to use them for the defence of their principles, their faith, and their country. They should not show their backs to the foe in a battle. They should live and act according to the three golden rules laid down by Baba Nanak. They should ever help the poor and the weak. They should always protect those who seek their help and protection. They should give up their previous castes. They now all belong to one caste, namely, the Khalsa. They must not eat *halal* meat, that is, the meat of animals killed in the Muslim fashion. Instead they should use *jhatka* meat— an animal killed with one blow. They must keep away from tobacco and wine.

'They must not worship idols, cemeteries or cremation grounds. They must not worship gods and goddesses. They should worship and believe only in one God. They should rise early, four hours before sunrise, bathe, read or recite the prescribed hymns of the Gurus, and meditate on God. They should be honest and truthful. They should ever trust in God and do the right. They should set apart a tenth part of their income for the Guru's cause and acts of charity.'

After that he desired his Beloved Five to prepare the *amrit* as he had done. When it was ready, he stood up before them with folded hands. He begged them to baptize him, to give him the *amrit*, in exactly the same way as he had baptized them. They were astonished at such a strange request. They hesitated, but the Guru said, 'Why do you hesitate? As I am your Guru, you collectively should be my Guru. You are to be my Khalsa, my other self, my beloved Ideal, and, therefore, quite competent to take my place after me. My Dear Ones, I have given you my form, my glory, and my appearance. I name you the Khalsa. There is no difference between you and me. I am now your *chela* or disciple. Baptize me as I have baptized you. Make me a Singh as I have made you Singhs.

The Beloved Five obeyed. They baptized the Guru just the same way as he had baptized them. His name was made to end in 'Singh'. It was changed from Gobind Das or Gobind Rai to Gobind Singh.

The Guru then invited others to take the *amrit*. Thousands of them, that is about 80,000, were baptized in a few days. They all became 'Singhs' or the Guru's Lions. The Guru also ordered that all those who called themselves Sikhs, should take the *amrit* and thus get themselves confirmed by receiving the new baptism. He further ordered that the ceremony of conversion to Sikhism, admission to the

Brotherhood of Saint-warriors and warrior-saints, would be conducted by a commission of five Beloved Ones.

Thus was born the Khalsa— a nation of saint-soldiers worshipping one God, friends and servants of man, and sworn foes of all tyrants, a Brotherhood in which all were to be equal in all respects, and in which all castes were united to form one nation—the Khalsa. The Khalsa was Guru Gobind Singh's type of the universal man of God—brave, fearless, and strong as a lion, sweet, humble, and loving as a woman, holy and pious as a saint, brother of all, striking fear in none, and himself afraid of none.

Through his baptism, Guru Gobind Singh poured his life into his Sikhs and invested them with his own personality. They came to be looked upon as models of physical power and beauty, and stateliness of character. The whole tone of national character was immensely changed. Sweepers, barbers, water-carriers, washermen and confectioners who had never touched a sword or shouldered a gun, who had for countless generations, lived as slaves of the so-called higher classes, were under the Guru's leadership, converted into brave warriors, ready to rush into the jaws of death at the bidding of their Guru, and leaders of armies before whom the Rajas and the Nawabs trembled with terror and dared not raise their heads.

HINDU RELIGION IN DANGER

We have seen how and with what aims Guru Gobind Singh created the Khalsa. Guru Nanak's object, as we know, was to abolish the distinction of caste and to bring all to the worship of that Supreme Being before whom all men, he declared, were equal. Guru Gobind Singh altogether prohibited the observance of caste-distinction within the Khalsa ; all Sikhs were equal and upon a level. The Brahmin who adopted his principles had no higher claims to eminence or superiority than the lowest *sudra* who swept his house. He had done something which no earlier Guru had done. He made men of all castes drink from the same vessel. This action of his was hailed by the low-castes and the out-castes who formed a vast majority of the people. But it was more than the high-caste people could bear. The Brahmins were upset more than all others. They had enjoyed the special rights and benefits of their special position for centuries. Now these rights and benefits were being taken away. They felt that they were being thrown down from their high positions. They were pained to find the low-castes and the out-castes being elevated to a position of equality with them. They did not, at all, like this levelling up and levelling down of the various castes and classes.

Anandpur was situated in the hill-state of Bilaspur. Guru Tegh Bahadur had built it on the land purchased from its ruler. There were about twenty hill-states. They were ruled by Rajput Hindu rajas who were Khatris by caste.

A party of Brahmins went to the hill-chiefs. They roused in them anger and fear against Guru Gobind Singh. They told them of the harm which his act of levelling up and levelling down of all castes was sure to cause to the Hindu religion and the high-castes. They said 'He is a revolutionary. He is out to wipe out, to sweep off, the Hindu religion. He is breaking up the back-bone of our religion. He has declared an all-out war on the caste-system. He is mixing the four castes along with the out-castes and uniting them all into one caste or class which he calls Khalsa. On becoming members of his Khalsa, all—high castes, low castes, and outcastes—become equal in all respects. His movement is becoming dangerously popular. If he is allowed to go unchecked, the Hindu religion and the Hindu culture will disappear altogether. It is your duty as Khatris to serve and save your religion. Moreover, even your own interests and safety demand speedy action against him. He is raising an army. If you don't check him in time, he will become too powerful for you all. He will drive you out of your kingdoms, and establish his own rule. O Rajas, not only your religion but also your kingdoms are in danger. . . . . Save them before it becomes too late.'

36

The hill-chiefs were already jealous and afraid of the Guru. They had tasted his steel at Bhangani. The Brahmins' words, therefore, filled them with alarm and

anger. They assured the Brahmins that they would soon take suitable and effective action against the Guru. The Brahmins went away highly pleased and well satisfied.

THE HILL CHIEFS TURN HOSTILE

The aim of Guru Gobind Singh in founding the Khalsa was to build up a nation that would be free from the then-prevailing evils of religion and society. But the rulers of the time thought that he was organizing a force to attack and destroy them. They regarded him, his Sikhs, and his teachings as an ever-growing danger to their power and religion. Every one of them began to look upon him as his mortal foe. A number of them met at Bilaspur. They reviewed the situation created by him. They discussed what steps should be taken against him. They decided to meet him before doing anything else. They said, 'Let us appeal to him to give up the path that he has chosen. If he refuses to pay heed to our appeal, we shall meet again and plan further action against him.

Accordingly, a deputation of the hill-chiefs arrived at Anandpur. Raja Ajmer Chand of Bilaspur was their leader. The Guru received them with due regard. A look at their faces revealed to him what was passing in their minds. He said to them, "Rajas, you are all caught up in a great misunderstanding. Your fears are baseless. Your objections against my creation of the Khalsa are ill-founded. They show that you do not understand the needs and the spirit of the times. I am not destroying your religion, or your society. I am trying to make it purer and stronger. I assure you that I have no idea at all of founding a kingdom. Your rule and kingdoms are not in any danger on my account. I do not want to deprive you of your thrones. I mean to make you stronger and safer. My aim is to end the rule of the cruel tyrants who treat you as their slaves. Need I remind you of what you and your people have to bear under their rule ? They force Hindus to become Muslims. They mercilessly butcher those who refuse to give up their religion. They dishonour your gods and goddesses. They pull down your temples and build mosques on their sites. Hence, it is they that are destroying your religion. They, not I, pose a danger to your religion. What is worse, they are out to destroy your homes. They seize your wives, sisters and daughters before your very eyes. You lack the courage to resist them, the courage even to resent their action. You bear all this, with mean meekness. Nay, you have fallen so low that you meekly give your daughters to your Muslim rulers. You do so because you are afraid of them and want to please them. I am deeply pained to see how low you have fallen. Are you not ashamed to call yourselves Rajputs ? Think of your great ancestors. Think of their fearless bravery and their lofty self-respect. Remember that it is their blood that runs in your veins. If you still possess an atom of that bravery and self respect, if you still have a trace of the ancient spirit of your race,

then listen to my advice.   Take the *amrit*.
Become members of the Khalsa Brotherhood.
You will acquire new strength and bravery.   Then
gird up your loins to face the tyrants in order to
free your, country and to elevate its fallen
condition.'

The hill-chiefs heard all this with lowered
heads. Then their leader, Raja Ajmer Chand of
Bilaspur, spoke out,   'O true king, what you say is
correct. It is true that we have fallen, fallen very
low indeed. But we are helpless. We can see no
way; out of our fallen state. The Turks are too
powerful for us. Who can withstand the Pathans
and the Mughals ?   Everyone of them can eat a
whole goat. We are nothing before them. Even if
we take your *amrit,* we can fare no better. We shall
still be no match for those mighty dreadful people.
Even you and your Khalsa will fail against them.
Your low-caste and out-caste soldiers are, at best,

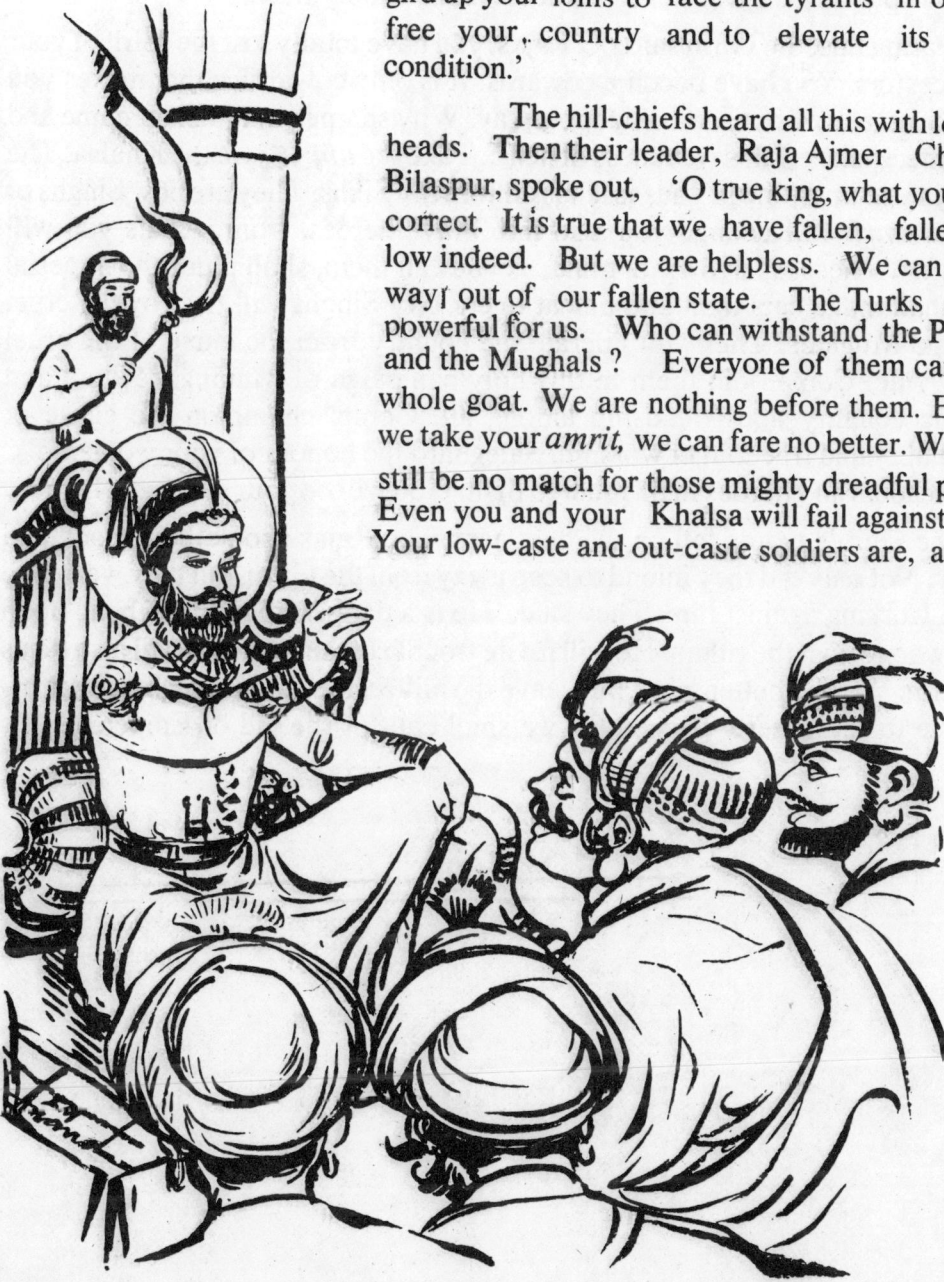

39

as cats fighting against tigers, or as tiny sparrows fighting against mighty hawks. Hence, it is best to make a virtue of necessity. We feel that discretion is really the better part of valour. We must endure what we cannot cure. We would advise you to give up your plans. You can never succeed. Take timely heed.'

On hearing this, the Guru said, 'O Rajas, you have totally lost the spirit of your mighty ancestors. You have become cowards. It is only cowardice that makes you think and behave in this miserable ignoble way. Why shame your ancient name and fame ? Come, shake off this weakness of heart. Take the *amrit,* join the Khalsa. The *amrit* will infuse a new life in you, as it has done in my Sikhs. They are now Singhs or Lions. The *amrit* will change you also into brave heroes, from jackals you will become tigers. These 'sparrows' of mine, as you call them, shall pluck the imperial hawks. I shall make cats fight and defeat tigers. My Singhs will destroy the cruel Pathans and Mughals. They will liberate the country from the curse of the cruel foreigners' rule. Come, join them in this holy campaign of winning freedom and establishing equality and friendship among all. Come, champion the cause of human equality and freedom of worship. Safeguard the honour of your womenfolk Come, be leaders and heroes in this sacred fight. God will be your guide and helper.

But the Guru's words fell on the deaf ears. The Rajas shook their heads and went away. Not only did they intend to keep away from the Guru, but they were also bent upon working against him. They said, 'He is a danger to us. He is bent upon starting a war against the rulers. He will invite trouble on himself. He will also do us infinite harm. We had better make him leave the hill-region and go to wherefrom his father came to settle here. If need be, we shall call for the aid of Emperor.'

THE HILL CHIEFS ON THE WAR PATH

Guru Gobind Singh needed peace for the success of his mission. He did not want war. But unluckily the high caste Hindus, especially the hill-chiefs, were bitterly against his programme of levelling up and levelling down of all classes and castes to bring them upon a level. They thought the Guru was destroying their religion and social structure.

So they started armed warfare against him. It began in 1700 A.D., and, with but slight pauses, continued to the end of the Guru's earthly life.

The hill-chiefs had chosen to become bitter enemies of Guru Gobind Singh. They regarded him as a constantly growing danger. They wished to get rid of him, the sooner, the better. But how to do that was the tough and perplexing question. The memory of Bhangani was yet alive in their uneasy minds. They hesitated to attack him ; for they fear that they might get another and more bitter defeat. All the same, they were making plans and plots to achieve their evil objective. They decided that every one of them should ever be on the lookout for a chance to harm the Guru. Then something occurred which they thought was a godsend for them.

One day, Guru Gobind Singh went out for hunting in the hills. He had only a small party of Sikhs with him. But they were all strong, selfless, and brave warriors, ever ready to lay down their lives for the Guru's sake. The bravest and strongest among them were Bhai Udhe Singh and Bhai Alim Singh.

Two hill-chiefs Balia Chand and Alim Chand, came to know of the Guru's presence in the hills. They also learnt that he had only a small party of Sikhs with him. Even these Sikhs, they were told, were scattered about in search of game. They thought, 'Here is a very good opportunity for us to get rid of the grave and ever-growing danger which the Guru means to us, to our race and religion. He has only a small party of Sikhs with him. They will be no match for our soldiers. We can easily defeat him and either capture or kill him. We shall, thereby, win name, fame and honour. Let us fall upon him suddenly.'

So thinking the two hill-chiefs quickly called out their armies. They made a sudden attack on a group of the Guru's companions. The latter were taken by surprise. But they did not feel unnerved or shaken. They stood their ground well and most resolutely. But it was a very unequal fight. They were too few to stand for long against the large body of the attackers. They were forced to retreat. But they did so in an orderly fashion, without any panic whatsoever.

41

At the time of this attack, Guru Gobind Singh was at some distance from the scene of the battle. Because of the hills and bushes all about him, he could not see what was happening. A Sikh came running to him and informed him of what had occurred. He rushed to the place of the encounter, raising loud shouts of 'Akal, Akal, Sat Sri Akal.'

His war cry was heard by the retreating Sikhs. It inspired them with fresh courage and resolve. They rallied round the Guru, raising the same war-cry of 'Akal, Akal, Sat Sri Akal.' Hearing this war-cry, other members of the hunting party rushed in from all sides. They all fell upon the hillmen. They began to cut down

the enemies as a woodcutter chops off twigs from a felled tree. The Guru discharged his arrows with fatal effect. The Sikhs fought with zeal, courage, skill, and determination. Both sides fought most desperately.

Balia Chand saw his men being destroyed by the Sikhs. He rushed forward to their aid. Bhai Udhe Singh, one of the bravest soldiers of Guru Gobind Singh's army, came forward to oppose Balia Chand. The other hill chief, Alim Singh, another of the bravest soldiers in the Guru's army, hastened to meet Alim Chand. The fight became severer still.

Alim Chand aimed a blow of his sword at Bhai Alim Singh. He received it on his shield. Then with his swift, strong return blow, he cut off the hill-chief's right arm. At this Alim Chand took to his heels. Balia Chand was thus left in sole command of the hill army. He was soon shot dead by Bhai Udhe Singh.

The hill troops saw that one of their cheifs had fled from the field and the other was dead. They at once took to flight. Thus the Guru and his Sikhs were left as the masters of the field. After the battle the Guru continued his hunting excursion.

The news of this battle and its result added to the hill-chiefs' fears. They thought it highly dangerous to allow the Sikhs to increase in strength and number. But they felt helpless. They realized that the Guru was too powerful for them. So they decided to complain to the Delhi government against the Guru and his Sikhs.

In their representation to the Delhi government they said, 'Guru Gobind Singh has established a new sect, distinct from the Hindus and the Muslims. He calls it his Khalsa. He has united the four castes into one. He welcomes even the out-castes. Even Muslims are becoming his Sikhs and members of the Khalsa. He invited us to join him. He said to us, "If you consent, you will get power and empire in this world and salvation in the next. You should rise in rebellion against the Emperor. I shall help you with my forces. As you know, the Emperor killed my father. I desire to avenge his murder. I assure you that you will win."

"But we did not think it proper to oppose our kind and just Emperor. We refused to accept his advice and suggestion. As a consequence, he is displeased with us. He has become our sworn enemy. We by ourselves cannot check or oppose him. He is too powerful for us. We, therefore, beg for the Emperor's protection against him. We, as loyal subjects of the Emperor, pray for help to expel the Guru from Anandpur. We beg to submit that if he is not checked in time, he will become a danger to the Emperor himself."

Emperor Aurangzeb was at that time engaged in warfare in the Deccan. So the hill-chiefs' representation was received by the subedar or viceroy of Delhi. It was then forwarded by him to the Emperor for orders.

THE HILL CHIEFS' AMAZEMENT

Guru Gobind Singh wanted and needed peace to carry on his mission. His aim was to prepare the people for winning freedom and equality in all spheres of life—religious, social, economic and political. As we have seen, the selfish and short-sighted hill-chiefs did not like his plans and campaign. They thought, 'He is sure to make us his first target. If he succeeds, we shall lose our kingdoms and our religion will be destroyed. They decided, therefore, to oppose him tooth and nail. They attacked him a number of times, without any provocation. They were defeated every time.

After a number of such defeats the hill-chiefs considered it prudent to make peace with the Guru. But their intentions did not undergo any change for the better. In their hearts they were still his bitter, sworn enemies. Hence the peace which they intended to make was to be only a temporary affair, a mere deception, a device to gain time. It was to be used as a cover under which they could plot, prepare and work against him.

Raja Ajmer Chand of Bilaspur was the most prominent among the hill-chiefs. Anandpur was in his territory. Naturally, therefore, he was more concerned and worried about the Guru's activities than the other chiefs. Hence, though outwardly professing to be at peace with the Guru, he was determined to expel him from Anandpur.

He decided to procced cautiously. He made a plan to find out the Guru's secrets. That was to be his first step in his preparations for war against the Guru. He thought that such knowledge would help him in defeating the Guru. Accordingly, he suggested to the Guru to let an ambassador of his be posted at his court. The Guru agreed most readily, for he wanted to live at peace with all. Raja Ajmer Chand, thereupon, sent a clever Brahmin, named Pamma, to the Guru's darbar, to serve as his ambassador. Really he was to work as a spy. He at once set himself to the task of finding out the Guru's secrets and collecting information which could be helpful in the planned fight against the Guru.

But he was careful to keep up appearances of friendship and cordiality. One day, at the instance of his master, he suggested to the Guru to go to Rawalsar near Mandi. He added, 'On the occasion of the approaching Baisakhi festival, all the hill-chiefs will gather there That is their usual custom. It will be an excellent

45

opportunity for having frank talks and cementing friendly relations.

The Guru was ever eager for peace and friendship. So he readily accepted Pamma's suggestion. In due course, he went there along with his family and a company of his Sikhs. All the hill-chiefs also gathered there. The Guru arranged a magnificent reception for them. They were charmed by his behaviour and engaging manners. They begged him to forget and forgive their past offences. They promised to behave well in future and to be ever on friendly terms with him. The Guru assured them that he had no enmity against them and that he would treat them as they deserved.

The Guru explained to them the main principles of the Sikh religion. He exhorted them to join hands with the Khalsa. 'Let us,' said he, 'make a united effort to free our country from the foreigners' cruel rule.' But they simply shook their heads. They declined to run any such risks. 'The Turks,' said they, 'are too strong for us. Your dreams can never be fulfilled. We are content with what we have, as what we are. We feel resigned to our lot as it is. We must endure what we cannot cure.'

The Guru tried his best to inspire them with courage and self-confidence, to put a new life in their dead bones. But they refused to accept his advice.

The Guru stayed at Rawalsar for a number of days. His morning and evening *diwans* or religious gatherings attracted large crowds. They were all provided good food in the Guru's free community kitchen. A large number of them were baptized and admitted to the Khalsa faith.

The wives of the hill-chiefs expressed a desire to see and hear the Guru. He received them in a separate tent. He gave them instructions suitable to their status and position. They were charmed to see and hear him. The Guru noticed that they were looking at him with deep admiration. Their eyes never left his face. He turned to the eldest among them and said that it was time for their departure. Most of the *ranis* (queens) did not wish to go away. But the eldest queen prevailed upon them to terminate their visit.

One of the princesses, named Padmani, daughter of the Raja of Chamba, later sent a letter to the Guru, with her father's permission. In it she asked some questions on spiritual matters and begged the Guru to answer them for her benefit. The Guru sent her suitable replies. The princess was delighted to read the Guru's letter. With her father's permission, she went again to see the Guru. When she bowed before him, he patted her on the shoulder with the sword. She said, 'I am your devout worshipper. Why have you not patted me with your hand?' He replied that he never touched any woman, except his wife. The princess bowed and went away.

One day the Guru was holding his darbar as usual. The hill-chiefs were all

46

present. A Sikh visitor offered to the Guru a number of weapons of his own make. Among them was a double-barrelled gun. The rajas admired the weapons and the skill of their maker. The Guru loaded the gun and said, 'Let a Sikh stand at a distance of a hundred yards. I want to see whether the gun can shoot a man at that distance.'

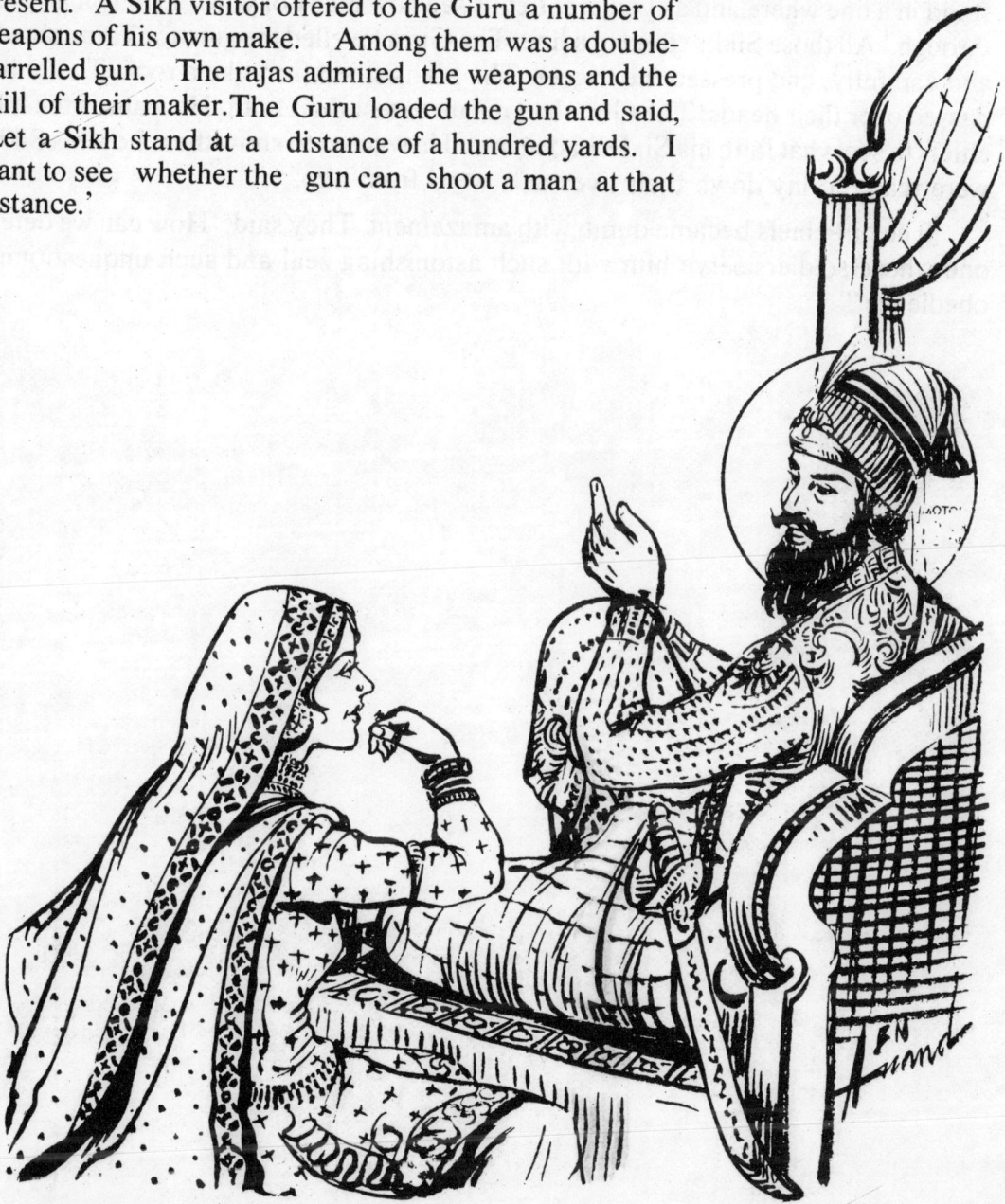

Thereupon several Sikhs rushed to serve as targets for the gun. Each of them tried to be in fornt of the rest. On seeing the struggle, the Guru said, 'Let all of you stand in a line where and as you are. Let us see how many of you the bullet can pass through.' All those Sikhs stood in a line. The Guru levelled the gun, took aim, slowly and carefully, and pressed the trigger. The Sikhs stood firm like a rock. The bullet passed over their heads. The Guru had meant to test their faith. He wanted the hill-chiefs to see what faith his Sikhs had in him. He wanted to show them how his Sikhs were ready to lay down their lives at a word from him.

The hill-chiefs became dumb with amazement. They said, 'How can we defeat one whose soldiers serve him with such astonishing zeal and such unquestioning obedience ?'

SAIYAD BEG

We have seen that the hill-chiefs had fought against Guru Gobind Singh a number of times, and had suffered crushing defeats. Finding themselves helpless against him, they had made a representation to Emperor Aurangzeb. The Emperor was at that time in the Deccan. The representation had been sent to him by the viceroy of *Sarhind* to whom it had been presented by the hill-chiefs.

While the hill-chiefs were awaiting the Emperor's orders on their petition, they got a chance to waylay and attack the Guru. He had gone to Kurukshetra on the occasion of a solar eclipse. He knew that a big religious fair was to be held there ; for such was the Hindu custom. One of his objects in going there was to carry the message of Guru Nanak to the people assembled there. His second object was to buy horses for his army.

Most of the hill-chiefs had also attended the fair at Kurukshetra. They saw that the Guru had at the most, a hundred soldiers with him. So they thought they could easily capture or kill him by falling upon him on his way back to Anandpur.

The decision was easy to make, but its execution was quite a difficult matter. The rats had decided to put a bell round the cat's neck—but who was to bell the cat ? No one could summon the needed courage. They were still debating the question, when they heard the news that two Muslim generals were near at hand. Their names were Saiyad Beg and Alif Khan. They were each in command of five thousand soldiers. They were on their way from Lahore to Delhi. The hill-chiefs decided to hire the two generals and send them against the Guru.

Raja Ajmer Chand met them for the purpose. Each was promised one thousand rupees a day. They agreed to perform the task for which they were hired.

Now, Saiyad Beg was a thoughtful man. He had a religious bent of mind. He became curious about the great person against whom he had been hired to fight. He made enquiries about the Guru. What he learnt filled him with admiration and respect. He decided not to fight against him. So he withdrew from the Muslim army.

The Guru was near Chamkaur Sahib when the Muslim hirelings fell upon him. The odds were extremely heavy against him. But he was not the man to lose heart even in the face of the heaviest odds. His faith in God and his self-confidence were infinite and unshakable. His Sikhs had unbounded faith and confidence in him. They were always joyfully ready to lay down their lives for him at his bidding. They fought for their faith and principles, for their Guru and God. How could mere hirelings stand against such soldiers of God ?

49

The battle raged in fury. The news of the hill-chiefs' wicked plans and act had reached Anandpur. Consequently, four hundred Sikh soldiers hurried from there to join the Guru. They arrived when the battle was raging in fury. They came raising the Khalsa war-cry of *'Akal, Akal, Sat Sri Akal.'*

The Guru's fast pouring and unerring arrows had rained death and destruction on the Muslim army. The dauntless fighting put in by the Khalsa army had made the hirelings waver in their hearts. At that time they heard the Khalsa war-cry raised

50

by the Sikh soldiers coming from Anandpur. This made their hearts sink still further. But they knew that the odds were over-whelmingly in their favour. So they continued to fight with desperate fury.

Saiyad Beg watched the fight for some time. What he saw filled him with wonder and admiration for the Guru and his Sikhs. He felt that it was not enough that he should abstain from fighting against that Faquir-soldier of Allah (God.) He should go over to him, kneel before him, become his follower, and help him actively in the unequal fight.

The battle was raging with great fury. It had come to a critical point. At that critical moment Saiyad Beg approached the Sikhs and said, 'Brothers mine, you believe in the Guru. So do I believe in him. I shall, therefore, fight on your side. Regard me as one of yourselves.' He joined the Sikhs. Many of his followers, who held the same views, accompanied him. Soon thereafter, he and his men were seen fighting against Alif Khan and his army.

Alif Khan had been wounded. His confidence had been shaken a good deal. Saiyad Beg's going over to the Guru took away what little courage he still had. He ordered a retreat. He was hotly pursued by the Sikhs and Saiyad Beg. On his return from the pursuit, Saiyad Beg alighted from his horse and went to pay his respects to the Guru. He had been a servant of Aurangzeb. Now he had given up that service. He now threw in his lot with the Guru and his Khalsa. He gave to the Guru all his wealth to assist him in his struggle against his enemies. He remained with the Guru as a trusted and powerful ally.

IMPERIAL ARMY DEFEATED

The hill-chiefs had become mortal enemies of Guru Gobind Singh. They had determined to kill him, or at least, to expel him from Anandpur. But all their attempts had proved ineffective. So, once again, they sent a representation to Emperor Aurangzeb through the Governor of Sarhind. In it they described the Guru as a dangerous enemy of Islam and Hindusim. They said that he was a sworn enemy of the Emperor and his loyal subjects like the hill-chiefs. They added that he wanted to convert all Muslims and Hindus to his faith and to establish his own rule in the country.

Emperor Aurangzeb had his own suspicions against the Guru. The hill-chiefs' representation and the report thereon of the governor of Sarhind served to confirm those suspicions. It aroused his fears. He ordered the governor to send a large army to fight, defeat, and capture or kill the Guru. Accordingly, the governor despatched an army of ten thousand under Saiyad Khan, Din Beg, and Painde Khan. The hill-chiefs joined them with their own armies which numbered above twenty thousand. The Guru had only seven thousand men, but they were men of altogether a different type.

The combined armies proceeded towards Anandpur. As they approached, the Guru prayed to God and lead his men to meet the advancing foe. A bloody battle began. Sahibzada Ajit Singh fought with wonderful skill and courage. The Guru discharged his arrows with fatal effect. The Khalsa army fell on their foes as do tigers on a herd of sheep. The invaders were falling fast before the onslaught of the Sikhs. Painde Khan then advanced and challenged the Guru. He asked the Guru to strike the first blow, but the Guru declined to be the aggressor even in such an encounter. Painde Khan shot two arrows in quick succession ; but failed to hit or hurt the Guru. He was about to retreat when the Guru challenged him to stop. The whole of his body except the eyes and ears were covered with steel. The Guru shot his gold-tipped arrow through Painde Khan's ear and brought him dead to the ground.

The Sikhs fought most valiantly. They held their ground wonderfully well against the overwhelming enemy. A number of Muslims were also fighting for the Guru. In fact, they were in the foremost rank of his army. One of them was Maimun Khan. Another was Saiyad Beg. They believed that the Guru was a true saint, a prophet of love and peace, and a soldier of God. They felt that he was being unjustly attacked. They said, 'It is not a war of Muslims against non-Muslims. It is a war of evil against good, of might against right. Our duty is clear. We must oppose evil and might. We must support and defend good and right. It is no sin to fight against the Muslim invaders.' So both fought valiantly against the imperial army.

Maimun Khan discharged arrow after arrow with mortal effect. Saiyad Beg killed everyone who came to oppose him. After a time, there occurred a severe single-handed combat between Saiyad Beg and a hill-chief. They attacked but repeatedly missed each other. At last Saiyad Beg cut off the hill-chief's head. Seeing this, Din Beg, a general in the imperial army, rushed to Saiyad Beg. A hand-to-hand fight ensued. Saiyad Beg was mortally wounded. He died praising the Guru and thanking God that He had given him a chance to make a good use of his life. The Guru came to the place where Saiyad Beg's body lay. He blessed the martyred hero and said, 'He has become immortal. He has gone to live for ever with the Father above. Those who die in a good cause never die.'

The battle continued to rage in great fury. The Sikhs, though greatly outnumbered, held their ground firmly and admirably.

Now let us have a speical look at Saiyad Khan, one of the generals leading the imperial army. He was the brother of Sayyid Budhu Shah's wife. As we know, Sayyid Budhu Shah and his wife were faithful followers of Guru Gobind Singh. The reader has already read much about them and the part which they played in the battle of Bhangani. From them Saiyad Khan had heard much about the Guru's spiritual powers and lofty principles. He had been, therefore, a great admirer of the Guru. On the battle-field he saw Muslims, like Maimun Khan and Saiyad Beg, fighting in the foremost ranks of the Guru's army. Naturally it made a strong impression on him. He felt a desire to meet and submit to the Guru. But his pride as a general of the imperial army stood in his way. He had come to conquer the Guru. What would the Emperor and his own comrades say if he submitted to one whom he had come to conquer and capture or kill ?

The Guru knew what was passing in Saiyad Khan's mind. He decided to end his mental struggle. He advanced towards him, smiling all the time. Saiyad Khan saw him approaching. He decided to do his duty as a general of the imperial army. He aimed a shot against the Guru but missed. He had never missed before. He advanced further in order to be nearer the Guru. The Guru smiled once more and said, 'Try again Saiyad Khan I am so near you. I hear that you are a good shot. Try once more.' Saiyad Khan, fired another shot, but missed again. The Guru advanced still nearer and said, 'Try once again, Saiyad Khan.' Saiyad Khan levelled his gun and took aim. But he could not pull the trigger. He was perplexed. A shiver ran through his body. The Guru smilingly said again, 'Try once more, I am so near you now.'

53

He who had come to conquer was himself conquered. He got down from his horse. He went up to the Guru with folded hands. He knelt beside the Guru and touched his feet with his forehead. He grasped the Guru's foot and said, 'I am your servant and slave, O Master. Accept me as such. I shall never fight against you or your Sikhs.'

The Guru bade him rise. He rose with light in his eyes and joy and love in his heart. The Guru conferred on him the gift of the true Name and the supreme reward of salvation. But unlike Saiyad Beg, Saiyad Khan did not actively assist the Sikhs. He fought no more against anyone. At the Guru's bidding, he retired to a lonely cave near Kangra. He passed his days there in thinking of God and the Guru. Later, when the Guru went to the Deccan, Saiyad Khan followed him and remained with him to the last.

After Saiyad Khan's having become the Guru's disciple, the command of the imperial army was taken over by Ramzan Khan who fought with great bravery against the Sikhs and caused much destruction.

On closely observing the field and the combat, the Guru saw that the odds were too heavy against him. Hence he decided to evacuate Anandpur. He retired into the fort. The Muslims plundered the city and the Guru's property. After that they proceeded in the direction of Sarhind. They encamped for the night a few kilometres from Anandpur. They were in high spirits. They had forced the Guru to quit the field and take shelter in his fort. A good half of the night was spent by them in feasting and merry-making. Then they lay down to sleep.

The Sikhs wanted to avenge their retreat. They obtained the Guru's permission to fall upon the imperial army during the night. The Guru's eldest son, Sahibzada Ajit Singh, was at their head. The Muslims were taken unawares. A scene of wild confusion followed. Hundreds were killed by the Sikhs. Others fled for their lives. All the booty which they had plundered from Anandpur, as well as their camp, fell into the hands of the Sikhs.

Of course the Emperor was much upset and dismayed to hear of the disaster to his army. He called upon his fugitive troops to account for their cowardice and defeat. They pleaded that the Sikhs had waylaid and taken them unawares. The Emperor then enquired what sort of person the Guru was. A soldier said, 'He is a young handsome man, well built and strong, a true saint, lover of God and His children, the father of his people, and in war equal to hundred thousand of men.' The Emperor was much displeased on hearing the praises of the Guru. He ordered the soldier to be dismissed from service at once. But he could not dismiss the soldier's words from his own mind. They sank deep into his heart. They came to him again and again. He felt much distressed thereby.

AURANGZEB'S INVITATION

We have seen how the imperial army led by Saiyad Khan and Ramzan Khan had been dealt with by Guru Gobind Singh. When the Emperor learnt how his army had fared, he was mad with rage. He declared that he would use his full strength against the Guru and put an end to his life and activities. But the court Qazi advised him patience. 'Let us use,' said he, 'a bit of state craft. Let us somehow persuade him to visit your court for a conference. If he be won over, he will be an excellent and most trustworthy ally.'

The Emperor accepted the Qazi's advice. It accorded well with his own innermost feelings. He had often said to himself. 'How good it would be if such a holy, strong man be won over and made a friend.'

He deputed the Qazi to convey the following message to the Guru, 'There is only one Emperor. You believe in one God, so do I. So your faith and mine are one and the same. I wish very much to meet you and have a frank talk with you. Come to me without any hesitation. Otherwise, I shall be angry and come to you. If you come, you will be treated as holy men are treated by kings. I have obtained this sovereignty from God. You should not oppose my wishes.'

Guru Gobind Singh knew quite well how Aurangzeb had treated many holy men, how he had treated his own father, brothers, and their families. He knew how he had treated the holy Guru Teg Bahadur. Hence it was not wise to trust him. He said to himself, 'I can well imagine what sort of treatment the cruel, crafty king will accord to me. It will be suicidal to fall into his hands.' He sent the following reply to the Emperor:—

'My brother, the Sovereign who has made you an emperor has sent me into the world to do justice. He commissioned you, too, to do justice. But you have forgotten your Creator's orders. You practise hypocrisy. In persecuting non-Muslims you are acting unjustly. You are violating God's orders. What you are doing, does not become a true believer in God, the Creator and Father of all. Hence I make bold to say that you do not believe in God. Until you give up ill-treating God's children, I cannot meet or talk to you. I cannot seek friendly ties with you.'

When despatching this reply to the Emperor, the Guru conferred a robe of honour on the Emperor's messenger.

On the other side, Raja Ajmer Chand and the other hill-chiefs were deeply distressed to see that the glory and power of the Guru and his Sikhs were increasing, day by day. On the top of that they learnt how the imperial army under Saiyad Khan and Ramzan Khan had fared. This news made them still more nervous and restless. They began to fear that the Guru would soon deprive them of their kingdoms. They got together and decided to send another petition to the Emperor. In this petition they implored the Emperor to send a strong army under able and worthy generals to crush the Guru. They assured him that they would join the imperial army with all their own troops.

57

Raja Ajmer Chand undertook to go and present the petition to the Emperor. The latter was at that time in the Deccan. Raja Ajmer Chand proceeded thither to present the petition to him. By the time he reached there, the Emperor had received Guru Gobind Singh's reply to his invitation. That reply and the hill chief's petition made him feel that the Guru was becoming a real and powerful danger to the Mughal rule. So he ordered that all available troops under the Nawabs of Delhi, Sarhind, and Lahore be despatched against the Guru. He also called upon the hill-chiefs to help the imperial army in every way. At the same time he desired that, at the conclusion of the campaign, the Guru should be captured and brought before him.

The Nawab of Delhi said that he could not spare any troops for the campaign against the Guru. The troops which he had were needed for the safety and defence of the imperial capital. However, the Nawabs of Sarhind and Lahore speedily marched towards Anandpur at the head of all their troops. The two armies met at Ropar. The armies of the twenty two hill-chiefs also joined them at that place. The Ranghars and Gujjars of the locality, who were Muslims, also joined the invaders there.

The Guru was thus faced with overwhelming odds. But he did not feel the least distrubed. He had unshakable faith in God whose soldier he was. The Sikhs had full confidence in their Guru. They were prepared to die fighting for him. So they boldly waited for the combined armies.

The invaders appeared in due course. The battle raged in great fury. The two Nawabs were astonished to behold the slaugher of their soldiers at the hands of the Sikhs. They had counted on an easy victory. But all their expectations were coming to a speedy ruin. Nine hundred Muslims and more than that number of hillmen were killed on the first day. The allied armies fared still worse on the following day. The Guru was ever in the hottest part of the battle. Every effort was made by his enemies to kill him. But he, as he said, wore the armour of the All-steel, the Immortal Lord. Bullets whistled past his ears, but did not hurt him. Fierce fighting went on for a long time. Both sides suffered heavy losses, but the Guru's enemies were by far the worse sufferers. It began to look impossible for the allied armies to defeat the Sikhs in the open battle-field. Still the fighting went on for many days.

BHAI KANHAEEYA

Among the Sikhs at Guru Gobind Singh's darbar was one named Bhai Kanhaeeya. He was a resident of village Sodra in the district of Gujjranwala, now in Pakistan. He was a devout and peace-loving Sikh. He had a tender and compassionate heart. He was ever busy in doing whatever service he found a chance to do. Because of his love for peace and service, and his tender-hearted disposition, he was averse to becoming a soldier and engaging in bloodshed. Therefore, he had not joined the Guru's army of saint-soldiers by taking *amrit*. But he was far from being a coward or an idler. He learnt the art of rendering first-aid to the injured and wounded. He gathered around him a band of persons eager to engage in such service, and organized them into an ambulance corps. Whenever fighting took place, he would take his ambulance band into the battle-field, and go about serving water and giving other help to the wounded, dressing their wounds and carrying them to his camp for further serice and treatment.

At the conclusion of one day's fighting, some Sikhs appeared before the Guru and said, 'O true king, a Sikh named Kanhaeeya is helping the Turks, our enemies against whom we are fighting. We wound and fell them, thus we make them incapable of fighting against us. But he goes and gives them water and other help. He makes them well and fresh. Hence they are soon ready to fight against us once again. He is thus undoing our work. He is thus helping the enemy. He should be ordered to desist from doing this.'

On hearing this, the Guru sent for Bhai Kanhaeeya. The latter appeared before the Guru in no time. The Guru said to him, 'Kanhaeeya, what have you been doing? I am told that you go about helping and serving the enemy. Is it true?'

'No, true king,' said Bhai Kanhaeeya. 'I have never given any help or done any service to an enemy. My brothers here are mistaken.'

'O true king,' said the complaining Sikhs, 'we are not mistaken. He is telling a lie. With our own eyes we saw him giving water and help to the enemy.'

'Well, Kanhaeeya,' said the Guru with a smile, 'I know you very well. I believe you to be incapable of telling a lie. But these my Sikhs are also incapable of making false statements. Come, tell me the whole truth.'

Bhai Kanhaeeya replied, 'From their point of view, what my brothers here say is true, yes, it is true that I have been giving water and help to those who are called

Turks as freely as to those called Sikhs. But in reality, I served no Turks or Sikhs. I was serving you alone, O true king.' 'Me?' said Guru Gobind Singh. 'How?'

'Thus, O true king,' replied Bhai Kanhaeeya. 'You have told us. "If you clothe a naked person, you clothe me. If you feed a hungry person, you feed me thereby. If you give water to a thirsty man, you give water to me." These words of yours have been engraved on my heart. They have gone deep

my mind. When I saw wounded soldiers, Sikhs and Muslims, lying on the ground, panting and thirsty, I saw not them but you, O true king. I saw you in every one of them. Hence, I gave water and help to none but you, my Lord.'

'Well done, Kanhaeeya,' said the Guru. 'You have been acting in the true Sikh spirit. As long as a Turk bears arms and fights against us, he is our enemy. But as soon as he falls wounded, on the ground, he ceases to be our enemy. He becomes a man, a son of the Father above. He deserves help and sympathy. My Sikhs should help and serve the wounded, be they Sikhs or Turks. My Sikhs should not chase and harm those who surrender their arms or fly from the field of battle.''

The Guru then gave a pot of ointment to Bhai Kanhaeeya and said. 'Carry on the good work. In addition to giving water to the wounded, dress their wounds. Then take them to a safe place for further service and treatment. Do this and your name will live in the world. God will be highly pleased with you.'

His followers called Sewapanthis, form an orthodox and honourable sect of Sikhs. They live by honest labour and accept no alms or offerings of any description.

It is said that the founder of the Red Cross got his inspiration from Bhai Kanhayeea's story as told above.

FAREWELL TO ANANDPUR

Aurangzeb had decided to put an end to Guru Gobind Singh's life and activities. He ordered the viceroys of Sarhind and Lahore to march against the Guru. They attacked Anandpur in 1701. All the hill-chiefs joined them with their armies. The Ranghars and Gujjars of the locality who were Muslims also joined the attackers. The Sikhs had to face overwhelming odds. They fought as they had never fought before, and held their ground against the repeated attacks of the Hindu and Muslim armies.

The Viceroys of Lahore and Sarhind were struck dumb on witnessing the splendid spirit and bravery displayed by the Sikhs. They saw their soldiers being killed in large numbers. After a time, they lost all hope of ever being able to defeat the Sikhs in open battles. They decided to besiege the city, cut off all supplies, and thus force the Sikhs to surrender or to die of hunger. They acted accordingly.

After a time, the effects of the siege began to be felt in the fort. Those inisde the fort began to feel pangs of hunger and thirst. Elephants and horses died lingering deaths for want of food. Now and then, the Sikhs fell upon the enemy's camp at night and took away some supplies and provisions from there. But such supplies could not last for long.

The Sikhs bore the hardships of the siege with exemplary patience and fortitude for three long years. But then they began to lose heart. They begged the Guru to evacuate the fort. But he would not listen to any such proposal. Overcome by fatigue, hunger and thirst, some of the Sikhs threatened to desert the Guru.

The besiegers came to know of the discontent which had begun to raise its head in the Guru's ranks. They decided to take timely advantage of it and thus end the war. Two messengers, a Brahmin and a Sayyid, were sent to the Guru. They were to say to him, 'The Hindu hill-chiefs and the Muslim Viceroys swear by the cow and the Quran, respectively, and give you the following promise. "If you evacuate the fort and go away, you will not be harmed in any way. You may even come back after a time." We assure you that the solemn oaths will be sincerely and fully kept and honoured.'

The messengers went to the Guru. They delivered the besiegers' message to him. At the same time, they swore by the cow and the Quran that the besiegers were sincere in their offer.

The Guru refused to put faith in these oaths. He said, "The hillmen have broken their solemn oaths many a time in the past. They are sure to do the same now and even in future. As for the Mughal Viceroys, they can be no better than their Emperor. Everyone knows how he treated his own father, brothers, and their families. I can trust neither the hill-chiefs nor the Truks.'

A number of Sikhs, however, were in favour of accepting the besiegers' offer. They went to the Guru's mother. They begged her to persuade him to accept the offer. She advised him accordingly. He tried to convince her that no reliance could be placed on the besiegers' oaths. But she was not convinced. Thereupon, he agreed to demonstrate the correctness of his opinion.

He said to the messengers, 'I shall evacuate the fort on one condition. The besiegers should first allow me to remove my movable property. Go, get their consent, and then come to convey it to me.'

They went away and soon returned to inform the Guru of the besiegers' consent. The Guru told them that he would send out his property that night.

The messengers went away. Under the Guru's orders such things as old shoes, torn clothes, horsedung, sweepings, and rubbish of all sorts were collected and packed in sacks. Thses sacks were to be the Guru's 'property' intended to be removed. They were covered with bright coloured cloth and loaded on the back of bullocks. Burning torches were tied to the bullocks' horns so that their departure and progress might be easily observed. Thus loaded, the bullocks were led out of the fort at the dead of night. As they approached the besiegers, the latter at once fell upon them to plunder the Guru's 'property'. When they found what the 'property' consisted of, they were filled with sorrow and shame. They had broken their solemn oaths and what had they attained!

The siege was, of course, continued. The condition of the besieged Sikhs grew worse, day by day. But they bore all hardships with patience and fortitude. Then came a letter in Aurangzeb's own handwriting. It said, 'I have sworn on the holy Quran not to harm you. If I do, may I not find a place in God's court hereafter ! Cease war-fare and come to me. If you desire not to come hither, then go withersoever you please. No harm shall be done to you.'

The letter was delivered to the Guru by a Qazi. The latter added that the hill-chiefs had sworn by the cow that they would not harm the Guru in any way. The Guru, thereupon, told the Qazi that he had no faith in the oaths and pledges of either the hillmen or the Turks. They were sure to be broken.

The Qazi went back. The siege was continued. The hardships of the besieged were becoming unbearable. So much so that a group of Sikhs decided to go away even against the Guru's wishes and advice. At that he said to them, 'All who want to leave, should give in writing that I am not their Guru and they are not my Sikhs.' A few hundred Sikhs wrote the 'disclaimer' and went away.

After a time, the Guru's mother became in favour of going away with her daughters-in-law and grandsons. At last, the Guru yielded to his mother's wishes. He agreed to evacuate the fort. Accordingly, he, his family, and his remaining Sikhs left the fort at midnight. That was on December 20, 1704. The night was dark and bitterly cold. A piercing cold wind began to blow. Soon it began to rain.

The besieging Hindu and Muslim armies learnt that the Guru and his Sikhs had evacuated the fort. They followed them, forgetting all their solemn oaths and pledges. They overtook the Guru and his party near the bank of the Sarsa stream. The night was dark. A bitter cold wind was blowing. The Sarsa was in flood. To cross it was very difficult indeed.

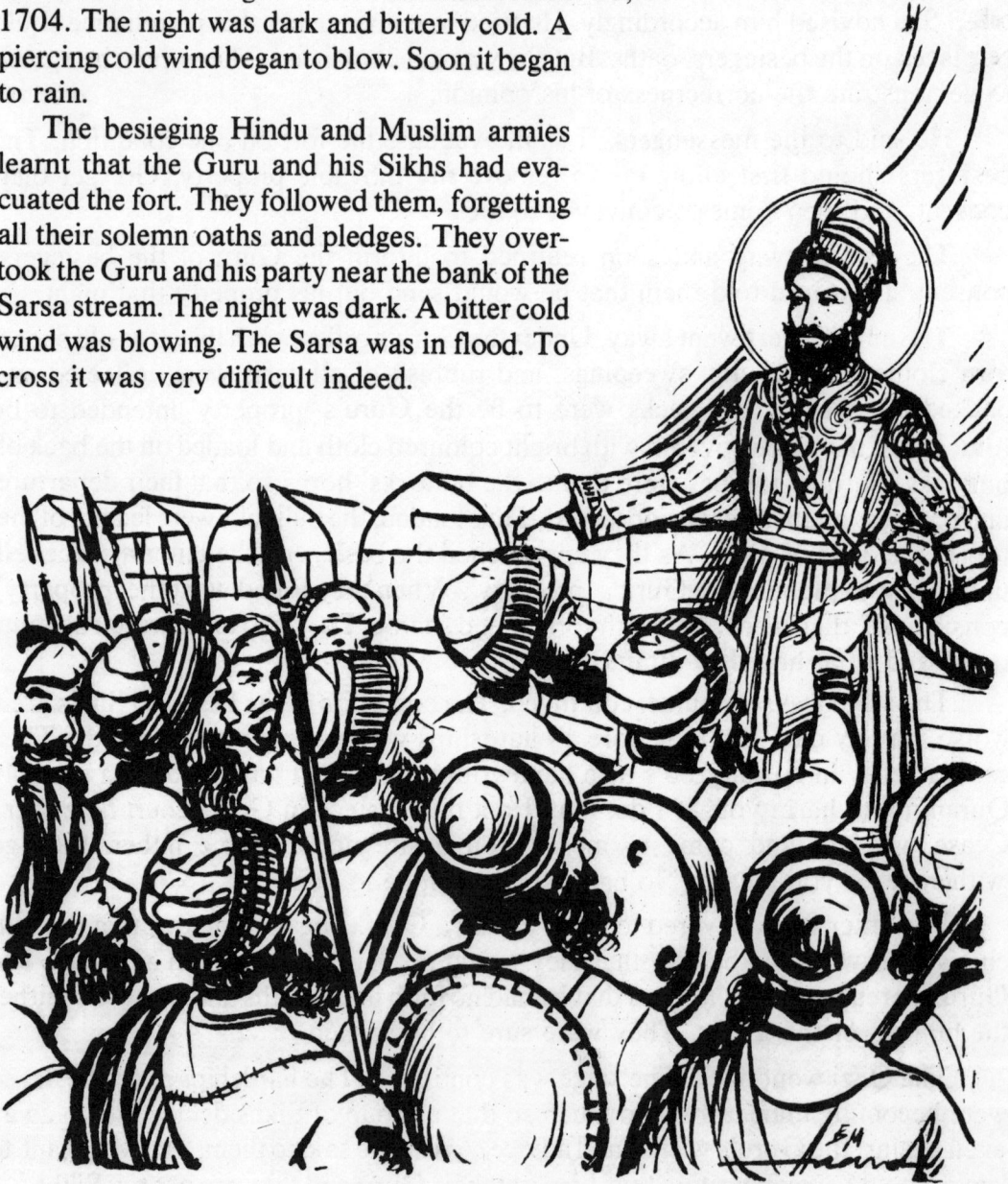

The Hindu and Muslim armies fell upon the Sikhs. There was hard fighting in the darkness and rain. In the confusion which ensued, all the Guru's baggage, including some very precious manuscripts, was lost in the waves of the Sarsa. Many Sikhs were killed. The rest succeeded in crossing the flooded stream. The Guru was separated apart from his family. His two elder sons, Baba Ajit Singh and Baba Jujhar Singh, accompanied him. His mother and two younger sons, Baba Zoraver Singh and Baba Fateh Singh were separated from the main party. What happened to them will be related in the next chapter. The Guru, along with his two elder sons and forty Sikhs went to Chamkaur Sahib in the district of Ambala. His five dear Ones were among the said forty Sikhs. His wives, Mata Sundri and Mata Sahib Kaur, stayed for the night in the house of a Sikh at Ropar. From there they went to Delhi on the following day in the company of that Sikh.

MURDER OF INNOCENTS

We have seen that when Guru Gobind Singh evacuated the fort of Anandpur, the Hindu and Muslim besigers forgot their solemn oaths, and fell upon him near the Sarsa stream. As said already, in the confusion which resulted from that attack, the Guru's mother, Mata Gujri, got separated from him and his Sikhs. His two younger sons. Baba Zoraver Singh and Baba Feteh Singh, were with her. In the biting winter wind of early dawn, she travelled as chance directed her. Her path lay through a thick jungle. Some way off, she met a Brahmin named Gangu. He had once been a cook at the Guru's house. His village Kheri was nearby. He offered to give her shelter in his house. She accepted his offer and went to his house along with her two grandsons.

The Brahmin proved to be a cheat. At night he stole Mata Gujri's saddle bag containing valuables and money. When she found the bag missing, she enquired about it from her host. Thereupon he flew into a rage. He said that he had been suspected and insulted. He at once went to the Muslim Headman of the village. He said to him, 'The Guru's mother and two sons have just come to my house. We both can earn a large reward by handing them over to the authorities!

The two went to the Muslim official of Morinda. They reported to him about the Guru's mother and sons. He was glad to hear the news. Taking a party of armed soldiers with him, he went to the Brahmin's house. He arrested Mata Gujri and her grandsons, and took them to Nawab Wazir Khan, the Governor of Sarhind. This happened on December 24, 1704.

The Nawab of Sarhind ordered them to be confined in a tower of his fort. They had to pass the cold December night with the bare, hard floor as their bed. Next day, that is on December 25, 1704, the Nawab ordered the children to be brought before him. When they took leave of their grandmother, she said, 'My dear children, keep to the ideas and examples of your grandfather and father. Don't say or do anything that may tarnish the name of the Guru. May God be your guide and helper !

The two brothers were taken to Nawab Wazir Khan's court. On reaching there, they shouted loudly, in one voice, *'Wahiguru ji ka Khalsa Sri Wahiguru ji ki Fateh.'* All eyes were turned in their direction. Their slim bodies their calm bright faces, and their fearless appearance won the admiration of all present in the court. Sucha Nand, a Brahmin minister of the Nawab, advised the younger boy to bow before the Nawab.

'No', said Baba Zoravar Singh 'We have been taught to bow before none but God and the Guru. We will not bow before the Nawab, come what may.'

This bold, unexpected reply astonished everybody. Even the Nawab could not help admiring the brave little ones. Then he said to them, in a soft voice, 'Children, your father and two elder brothers have been killed at Chamkaur. They were infidels and deserved that fate. But you are lucky. Good luck has brought you to an Islamic darbar. Embrace Islam, become one with us. You will be given wealth, rank, honour, and every form of pleasure. When you grow up, I shall marry you to beautiful daughters of respectable chiefs. You will live happy lives. You will be honoured by our great Emperor. If you say "No" to my offer, you will be treated as infidels are treated. You will be put to death with tortures.'

Baba Zoravar Singh, looking at his younger brother, said in a whisper, 'My brave little brother, the time to sacrifice our lives has come. What do you think should be our reply?''

Baba Fateh Singh, who had seen only six winters, replied, 'Brother dear, our grandfather gave his head but stoutly refused to give up his faith. We should follow his example. We have received the baptism of the spirit and the two-edged sword. We are the Guru's lions. Why should we fear death? We should most readily and gladly give up our lives for the sake of our faith. I am prepared to embrace death rather than to embrace Islam.'

Baba Zoravar Singh was mightily pleased to hear the brave words of his younger brother. He said 'Bravo dear, we should preserve the good name and honour of our family. The blood of Guru Arjan Dev, Guru Har Gobind, Guru Tegh Bahadur, and Guru Gobind Singh runs in our veins. We should not do anything unworthy of our family.'

Then Baba Zoravar Singh raised his voice and said, 'O Nawab, you say that our father has been killed. That is a black lie. He is alive. He has yet to do a good deal of work in this world. He has to shake your empire to its roots. Know that we are sons of him who, at my age, sent his father to sacrifice his life in order to safeguard freedom of conscience and worship. We hate and reject your religion. We reject your offers of high positions and worldly pleasures. It has been the custom of our family to give up life but not to give up faith. Our choice is made. Let your sword do its work. We invite you to do your worst.

These words were enough to inflame the haughty, bigoted Nawab. But Sucha

Nand Brahmin chose to pour oil over the fire. He said, 'So such is their behaviour at this tender age. What will it be when they grow up? They will follow their father's example, and destroy imperial armies. The offspring of a cobra should be crushed in time.'

The Nawab whispered to him, 'What you say is true and wise. But I very much desire to make them embrace Islam. They will be valuable additions to our community. There need be no hurry. They are in our power. They cannot run away. Let us give them time to think and consult with their aged grandmother. We shall try again tomorrow to make them yield.'

Then, turning to the two brothers, he said, 'I don't want to act in haste. I give time to think over the matter. Be wise and decide in favour of accepting my offer. You will live in peace, pleasure, and honour. If you refuse, you will be given such tortures that your cries will be heard far and wide. Then you will be cut into pieces like fodder.'

Then he ordered them to be taken back to the tower. Next day, that is on December 26, 1704, they were taken again to the Nawab's court under a heavy guard. Before they left, their grandmother again exhorted them to adhere to their faith, come what might. They assured her that they would act in a way worthy of her grandsons.

On entering the court, they shouted louder than they had done on the previous day, *'Wahiguru ji ka Khalsa Sri Wahiguru ji ki Fateh.'* In the court the same threats were given and the same offers were made as on the previous day. They stood firm and gave the same answers as on the previous day. Sucha Nand Brahmin again pressed the Nawab to give immediate orders for their death. But the latter again decided to give them more time to think over. He still had hopes that they would yield. So they were again taken back to the tower.

Next day, that is on December 27, 1704, they were again taken to the Nawab's court. There the same offer was made by the Nawab and rejected by them. When the Nawab was convinced that they would not yield, he gave orders that they should be bricked alive and then beheaded. On hearing this, the Qazis and other mean people like Sucha Nand Brahmin said aloud, 'That is as it should be.' But most of those present in the court set with their heads bent low, and their eyes wet and fixed on the ground. Then Sher Mohammed, Nawab of Malerkotla, said 'Nawab Sahib, your order is against the rules of Islam. The Muslim law forbids the slaughter of tender-aged innocent children. These two have done no wrong. The rules of our religion clearly lay down that a son should not suffer for acts done by his father, and that every one is answerable for his actions. So, under the laws of our religion, these boys should be allowed to go unharmed. They should not be punished for what their father has done.'

The Sikhs have always remembered this protest of the Nawab with gratitude, and throughout their troubled relations with the Muslim powers, they have always spared the house of Malerkotla from their attacks.

But the Qazis said, 'What do you know of the holy law ? How can you claim or pretend to know it better than we. The holy law gives them choice between Islam and death. Let them choose as they like.'

The Nawab expressed agreement with the Qazis. Two Pathan brothers were sitting near him. He said to them, 'You know that your father was killed by these boys' father. You may avenge his death. I hand them over to you. Kill them in a manner that I order.'

But the Pathans shook their heads and said, 'Our father was killed on a field of battle. He was not murdered. If these boys were full-grown men, armed with weapons, we would certainly have fought with them and killed them. That would have been a proper revenge. We cannot strike these innocent, unarmed tender-aged children. They have done us no worng.'

The Nawab was rendered speechless. He turned to left and right, seeking someone willing to do the bloody act. But all hung down their heads as a sign of their unwillingness, as a sign of their pity for the children. At last, looking behind, he saw two Ghilzai Pathans. The Ghilzai tribe was notorious for its heartlessness and cruelty. These two Pathans offered to do the bloody deed. The boys were delivered to them. They led them away for execution.

Under the Nawab's orders, a part of the outer wall of the fort was pulled down. The two children were made to stand in the gap thus created. The Pathans stood nearby. They had drawn swords on their shoulders, tightly held in their right hands. Their faces were fierce, their eyes were red, and their lips were tightly pressed together. An offical from the Nawab's court was also present. He was there to see that the Nawab's orders were duly carried out. A Qazi, with a copy of the Quran in his hand, also stood nearby. Masons were ordered to erect a wall round the children. They were told, 'Take care that the bricks press well and tightly against their bodies.'

After each layer of the bricks, the Qazi urged the two to save their lives by accepting Islam. But they stood calm and firm. They were busy in reciting sacred hymns of the Gurus.

When they were buried in the wall up to the shoulders, the Nawab himself came there. He, too, urged them to accept Islam and thus save their lives. They simply shook their heads. Nawab made a sign to one of the Pathans. The Pathan cut off Baba Zoravar Singh's head with a stroke of his sword.

The Nawab said to Baba Fateh Singh, 'You have seen what has happened to your brother. I advise you, for the last time, to accept Islam. Otherwise your head will be rolling on the ground.' He replied, 'Be quick, despatch me after my dear brother, so that we may go together into the lap of our martyred grandfather, and int the presence of the Almighty Father.'

At a nod from the Nawab, the other Pathan cut off Baba Fateh Singh's head.

In Sarhind there lived, at that time, a Sikh named Todar Mal. He heard that Guru Gobind Singh's mother and two sons had been imprisoned by Nawab Wazir

Khan. Taking a large bag of gold coins with him, he hastened to the Nawab's court. His intention was to free them by paying as much as the Nawab would demand. But he arrived too late. The two brothers had been put to death by then. He visited the place where they had been bricked alive and beheaded. After paying homage to the two martyrs, he proceeded to their grandmother. With his eyes melting into tears, and in a voice choked with sobs, Todar Mal told her of her grandsons' martyrdom. On hearing this, she said, 'Well, have my darlings already gone to meet their martyred grandfather in the lap of God ? I had taken upon myself the duty of looking after them. They have gone. What have I to do here now ? O my soul, fly after them to the bosom of the Merciful Father.'

Saying this, she closed her eyes and began to repeat *Wahiguru Wahiguru.* Soon she was gone to meet her grandsons. Todar Mal touched her feet and sobbed in anguish.

Then he went to the Nawab. He sought his permission to cremate the three bodies. He was told, 'You may do so. But for the cremation you will need a piece of land. You will have to pay for it. You may have the requisite land by paying as many gold coins as placed closely together, would completely cover it.'

Todar Mal chose the site. He spread out gold coins to cover the whole piece of land that he required. He took out the two martyrs' bodies from the wall. He took out Mata Gujri's body from the tower. He took the three bodies to the site selected and purchased by him. He cremated them and later buried their ashes there.

On the spot where the three bodies were cremated was later erected a gurdwara named Joti Sarup. At the place where the two children were bricked alive and beheaded, stands the gurdwara called Fatehgarh Sahib. Nearby, at the site of the tower in which the three were kept imprisoned, and where Mata Gujri breathed her last, stands a gurdwara called Mata Gujri's Burj.

AT CHAMKAUR SAHIB

After evacuating Anandpur, Guru Gobind Singh proceeded towards Ropar. He soon learnt that a large Muslim army lay a few miles in front. He knew that the armies of the two viceroys and the hill-chiefs were pursuing him. He was thus between two formidable armies. He had only forty Sikhs and his two elder sons with him. He decided to change his course and go to Chamkaur. On reaching there, he occupied a mud-built house or *haveli*. It was located on a high spot and was in the shape of a fort. He posted soldiers to guard the four walls and the gate. With two Sikhs and his two sons, he held the top storey.

The Mughal armies arrived at nightfall. They surrounded the village. Early next day they began their attacks on the *haveli*. They were greeted, each time, with a volley of bullets and arrows. Each time they fell back after losing many of their soldiers. Two army officers, Nahar Khan and Gairat Khan. tried, in turn, to scale the wall of the *haveli*. They were cut down by the Guru. Another officer, Mahmud Khan, saved himself from the Guru's arrows by hiding behind a wall.

The imperial army then decided to direct all their efforts towards forcing open the gate. As they moved in that direction, a number of Sikhs went out to oppose them and defend the gate. They fought most valiantly and killed many of the attackers. At last, they were overpowered and slain. Then another batch of Sikhs came out and bravely engaged the attacker as long as they could.

This went on for a good part of the day. Then there was a slight pause. The Sikhs met and decided to request and prevail upon the Guru to make good his escape. 'If he goes,' said they, 'he can raise thousands to carry on the fight for sacred cause.' So they approached him to make the request. They found that the Guru's eldest son, Baba Ajit Singh, was standing, with folded hands before him. He was begging permission to go out and check the enemy's advance in the next attack, which was sure to come soon. 'Dear father,' they heard him say, 'you have named me Ajit or unconquerable. I shall justify your choice of my name. I shall not be conquered. I shall not yield. If I am overpowered, I shall die fighting like my brother Sikhs.'

The Guru embraced and kissed his son for the last time. He then bade him go into certain death. The Sikhs fell on their knees before the Guru and begged him to save himself and his two sons. But the Guru did not agree to do so.

Baba Ajit Singh, who was hardly eighteen bade farewell to his father, his

younger brother, and his brother Sikhs. Five Sikhs accompanied him. The attackers came on. They were engaged by Baba Ajit Singh and his five companions. Many of the attackers were cut down. At last, the six brave warriors were overcome and killed.

The Guru had been watching his son from the top storey, and admiring and rejoicing at his daring bravery and skill as a warrior. When he saw him fall, he thanked God that his son had proved worthy of His cause.

The Guru's second son, Baba Jujhar Singh now made the same request as his elder brother had made. The Guru took him in his lap. He kissed and patted him. Then he gave him a sword and a shield. 'Go my son,' said the Guru, 'and join your grandfather and elder brother, 'Go and wait for me there.'

Thus armed, this lad of fourteen years went out to face thousands of hard, well-trained, and far better armed Mughal soldiers. Two Sikhs accompanied him. Baba Jujhar Singh fought as valiantly as his elder brother had done. Many mighty soldiers fell under the sword of the child-warrior. Then he was overpowered. He died fighting to the last.

The Guru had been watching and admiring Baba Jujhar Singh's wonderful performance. When he fell, the Guru thanked God that his second son had also proved worthy of His cause.

The gate was attacked and defended in this way throughout the day. At night the Mughal army lay down to take rest. By then, besides the Guru's two sons, three of his five Beloved ones had been killed. Their names were Bhai Muhkam Singh, Bahi Sahib Singh, and Bhai Himmat Singh. Thirty two other Sikhs had also fallen. Only five Sikhs were left with him.

These five Sikhs met the Guru and said, 'We beg you to make good your escape. You will create thousands of Khalsa warriors. The Khalsa warriors will destroy the cruel, Godless tyrants.' The Guru shook his head. Thereupon, the Sikhs said, 'O true king, at the time of the creation of the Khalsa, you declared, 'The Guru is the Khalsa, the Khalsa is the Guru.'' We as the Guru Khalsa, order you to go. We hope you will excuse our adopting this role.'

The Guru was left with no alternative. He had to obey the Guru Khalsa. He seated his five Sikhs near him and proceeded to entrust the Guruship to them. Then he said, 'After me the Khalsa Panth shall be the Guru under the guidance of Guru Granth Sahib. Whenever five Sikhs assemble and remember or call me, I shall be with them. They shall be the priests of priests. Whenever a Sikh breaks any of the rules of the Khalsa conduct, five Sikhs can give him baptism afresh and grant him pardon.'

Saying this, the Guru went round them thrice. Then he laid his plume and crest in front of them, gave them his arms, bowed before them, and said aloud, '*Wahiguru ji ka Khalsa, Sri Wahiguru ji ki Fateh*.

The Guru Khalsa further decided that three Sikhs-Bhai Daya Singh, Bhai Dharam Singh and Bhai Man Singh— should accompany the Guru. Two Sikhs— Bhai Sant Singh and Bhai Sangat Singh—were to remain in the *haveli*. They were to hold it as long as there was breath in their bodies.

The Guru and his three companions left the *haveli* at the dead of night. It was pitch dark. Thick clouds covered the sky, here and there. There were occasional flashes of lightning. As they proceeded, Bhai Daya Singh said, 'O true king, here lies the body of Baba Ajit Singh.' The Guru looked at the body, blessed his martyred son and walked on. A moment later, Bhai Daya Singh said, 'Here lies the body of Baba Jujhar Singh.' The Guru looked in that direction, blessed his martyred son, and walked on. Bhai Daya Singh then said, 'O true king, I have a sheet with me. I wish to tear it into two pieces and cover with them the bodies of the two martyrs.'

The Guru said, 'The idea is good. You have my permission, but on one condition, you should first cover the bodies of my thirty five martyred Sikhs. They are my sons in spirit and equally dear to me. After that you may cover the bodies of these two martyrs, who are my sons in flesh.'

Bhai Daya Singh could make no reply. He bowed and held his tongue. They then proceeded on their risky course.

BEFRIENDED BY MUSLIMS

Guru Gobind Singh and his three companions left Chamkaur at the dead of December night. The Guru pointed to a star and said to his companions, 'We shall proceed in the direction of that star.' Because of pitch darkness, the Guru got separated from his companions. He travelled barefooted. His path lay through wild land covered with thorny bushes. His feet got pierced with thorns. Blisters also appeared on them. His clothes got torn by getting entangled with the thorny bushes. The night was pitch dark. A biting cold wind was blowing fast. Consequently he could not make much progress.

A short time before dawn he reached near a village named Kheri. There he was recognized by two Gujjars. These Muslims raised an alarm. He was forced to kill them. As the imperial army was after him, he could travel only by night. During the day he rested among clusters of thorny bushes. He had nothing to eat but the tender leaves of the plants. He had nothing but a clod of earth to rest his head on. But amid all these hardships, his heart and mind were as firm and unshaken as ever. When he lay down to sleep on the bare earth, his hand always grasped his drawn sword.

The Guru was travelling through the thorny wilds of Machhiwara. Feeling exhausted, one day, he lay down to take rest. His three companions had travelled in the direction of the star which had been pointed out to them by the Guru. They reached the same place. They found him asleep with a small earthen waterpot as a pillow under his head. They awakened him. They told him that the imperial army was in hot pursuit. It might be on them at any time. They must get out of its reach. But he would not walk as his feet were blistered, thorn-pierced, and painful. He told them to go away and take shelter in a neighbouring garden. But how could they go, leaving him there ? Bhai Man Singh lifted him on his back and carried him to a well in the garden. There he took water and bathed for the first time after many days. He felt much refreshed.

The garden belonged to Gulaba Masand, a resident of Machhiwara. He heard of the Guru's presence in his garden. He hurried to meet the Guru and offer him his services. He took the Guru and his companions to his house. He lodged them in the upper storey. But, as the imperial army was after the Guru, it was not safe for him to stay there for long. He had to move on soon.

In that village there lived two Pathan brothers named Ghani Khan and Nabi Khan. They had been in the Guru's service for some time. They came to know of his being in their village. They also heard of the risky situation in which he then was. They decided to help him. They went to him and offered him their services. They said to him, 'O true king, permit us to carry you to a safe place.'

Now when the Guru was in Gulaba's house, an old Sikh lady, named Gurdevi, came to see him. She had been spinning and weaving a piece of cloth for him. She had been, at the same time, praying that he might be pleased to visit her village to receive it. On hearing of his presence in her village, she went and offered the cloth to him. At the Pathan brothers' suggestion, he got the piece dyed blue. Then he got it made into a robe and a sheet. He thus got prepared a dress like that worn by a sect of Muslim faqirs.

The Guru put on the robe and the sheet. Thus disguised, he was borne in a litter. It was lifted by Ghani Khan and Nabi Khan in the front and by Bhai Man Singh and Bhai Dharam Singh in the rear. Bhai Daya Singh waved a *chauri*. Whoever questioned them was told that they were escorting the Uchch Pir. The expression 'Uchch Pir' meant a high saint, but it could also be interpreted as the Holy Saint of Uchch, a well-known Muslim sacred place near Multan (Pakistan).

They travelled in this way without any mishap. One day, however, they were overtaken by the pursuing party. Its commander suspected that the Uchch Pir was none other than Guru Gobind Singh. He questioned the escorting party about the identity of the Pir. He was not satisfied with the answers that he got. He sent for Qazi Pir Muhammed, who had once been the Persian tutor of the Guru. He asked the Qazi to identify the occupant. The Qazi said, 'Don't stop this great and holy passenger. Don't put him to any inconvenience. He is a high saint in union with Allah. Let him proceed unmolested.' The commander was satisfied. He made apologies to the Uchch Pir for having suspected and inconvenienced him. He begged the Pir to go whither he pleased. For this timely service the Qazi was given a *hukamnama* or an autograph letter of recommendation addressed to Sikhs in general. It is retained still by the Qazi's descendants and is shown by them, with great respect, to those who visit their house.

Thus escorted, the Guru reached Hehar in the Ludhiana district. In that village lived Mahant Kirpal Das. He was the same Udasi Mahant who had distinguished himself in the battle of Bhangani. He welcomed the Guru most devoutly and cordially. Ghani Khan and Nabi Khan were permitted to go back home. Each was given a pair of gold bracelets and a *hukamnama* or an autograph letter of recommendation addressed to Sikhs in general. In that *hukamnama* it was written that Ghani Khan and Nabi Khan were dearer to the Guru than his own sons. The families of these Muslim friends of the Guru still retain the said autograph letter granted to them by the Guru and show them with respect to those who visit their house.

Mahant Kirpal Das was eager to save the Guru. But he had heard the imperial orders against helping or sheltering him. He feared that some local official might come to know of the Guru's stay at his house. The Guru read his mind. He decided to move on. The Mahant acted as one of the bearers of the Guru's litter for a few kilometres. Then he was allowed to go back.

From Hehar the Guru moved on to Jatpura. There he was met by a Muslim named Rai Kalha. He was a rich and important person and the Headman of Jagraon and Rai Kot. He was a devout admirer of the Guru. He knew of the imperial orders against helping or sheltering the Guru. But the knowledge did not deter him from serving the Guru. He took him to his house and treated him with most loving hospitality.

The Guru asked him to send somebody to Sarhind to get information about the fate of his mother and sons. The messenger sent by Rai Kalha returned in a few days. He brought the sad news that the children had been done to death, and that his mother had died of the shock which she got on hearing of their death. He received the news with perfect composure. Checking his tears and turning his sorrow into a strong resolve, he said, 'No, no, my sons are not dead. They refused to give up their religion and laid down their lives instead. They have become immortal. They shall live for ever. The town of Sarhind, where none raised a voice of protest against the cowardly murder, has invited its doom. It shall perish. The Nawab of Malerkotla, who tried to dissuade the Nawab of Sarhind from this atrocious act, has perpetuated his dynasty. My sons have conquered Death and have become immortal.' Saying this, he knocked out a shrub with his arrow and said, 'The enemy shall be uprooted like this.'

ZAFARNAMA

After a short stay at Jatpura, as Rai Kalha's guest, the Guru moved on to Dina, in district Ferozepur. At that place he was lovingly served by three brothers named Shamira, Lakhmira, and Takht Mal. The Nawab of Sarhind learnt of this. He sent strict orders to Shamira, telling him to arrest the Guru and bring him to Sarhind. Shamira ignored the orders.

While staying at Dina, Guru Gobind Singh wrote a letter to Aurangzeb. It was in reply to a summon received from the latter. It was written in Persian verse. He called it *Zafarnama* or an Epistle of Victory. A few sentences therefrom are given below :—

'I have no faith whatsover in your oaths to which you took God as witness. I do not have a particle of confidence in you.'

What happened at Chamkaur is that forty men reduced to hunger could do nothing when thousand fell on them, suddenly and unawares. The oath-breakers attacked them abruptly with swords, arrows, and muskets. At last, many were killed on both sides and the earth was covered with blood. Corpses lay in heaps—The brave (Sikh) warriors fought most valiantly, not caring for their lives. But how could forty, even braver than the bravest, succeed against a countless host ? When the sun set, God, my Protector, showed me the way to escape from my enemies. Not even a hair of my head was touched.'

'O faithless man, you are given to swearing false oaths, which you never keep— you keep no faith and observe no religion. You do not know God and do not believe in Muhammed. He who has regard for his religion never acts against his promise. You have no idea of what an oath on the Quran means, nor do you have any faith in God. Were you to take a hundred oaths on the Quran, I would not trust you even in the slightest—Everybody should be a man of word, and not have one thing in the heart and quite another on his lips. If you come to village of Kangur, we shall have an interview. Come to me so that we may speak to each other and that I may utter kind words to you.'

'If you have any belief in God, delay not in this matter. God never ordered you to oppress any person—Smite not anyone mercilessly with your sword, or a sword from above shall smite you and spill your blood. O man, do not be reckless, fear God. He is the Protector of the weak and miserable, and Destroyer of the reckless— What though my four sons have been killed ? The coiled cobra still remains. I am still alive and unconquered. What is the use of putting out a few sparks, when you raise a mighty flame in their place ? Do not spill the blood of men, for your own blood will as surely be spilt by death—If you rely on men and money, my eyes are fixed on the Almighty God.

'I would have gone many times to you had your promise been kept when my bullocks were plundered at Anandpur. As you did forget your word on that day, so will God forget you. God will, for certain, punish you for the evil deed which you designed—I do not think you know God, since you have done acts of oppression.'

'On that account the great God knows you not and will not receive you with all your wealth. Had you sworn a hundred times on the Quran, I would not have trusted you in the slightest even for a moment. I will not enter your presence, not travel the same road with you—'

'Fortunate are you, Aurangzeb, king of kings, expert swordsman and rider. You are well built and intelligent—You are generous to your co-religionists and prompt to crush your enemies—You are, monarch of the world, bit far from you is religion.—'

'What can an enemy do when God, the Friend, is kind ? You are proud of your army and wealth. I repose my trust and confidence in the kindness of the King of all kings. Be not heedless. Even though you are strong, oppress not the weak. Lay not the axe to your kingdom. When God is a Friend, millions of enemies cannot do any harm.'

This Epistle of Victory was entrusted to Bhai Daya Singh and Bhai Dharam Singh, the two of the Beloved Five who had survived the battle of Chamkaur, and accompanied him during his wanderings. They were directed to deliver it to Aurangzeb who was then at Ahmadnagar in the Deccan. The two dressed themselves as *hajis* or Muslim pilgrims bound for Mecca. After meeting many hardships on the way, they reached Ahmadnagar, and delivered the Guru's letter to Aurangzeb. At that time the Emperor was lying on his death bed, and was feeling that his end was near. The letter which he dictated for his sons then show that he was feeling intense remorse for his past. In one of the letters he said, 'I carry with me the fruits of sins and imperfection. I have committed numerous crimes and know not with what punishment I may be seized.'

The Guru's letter must have called up before his fevered, agitated mind clear pictures of his sins and crimes against the Guru, committed in violation of his oaths on the Quran. It told him what he should expect from God and the Prophet. It had a strong effect on the dying Emperor. It softened his heart and filled him with repentance. It deepened his remorse for the past and his fear and anxiety about the future.

He treated Bhai Daya Singh and Dharm Singh with courtesy and kindness. He asked them to appeal to the Guru on his behalf and prevail upon him to come and visit him, and speak to him 'the kind words' which he had promised to do in his letter.

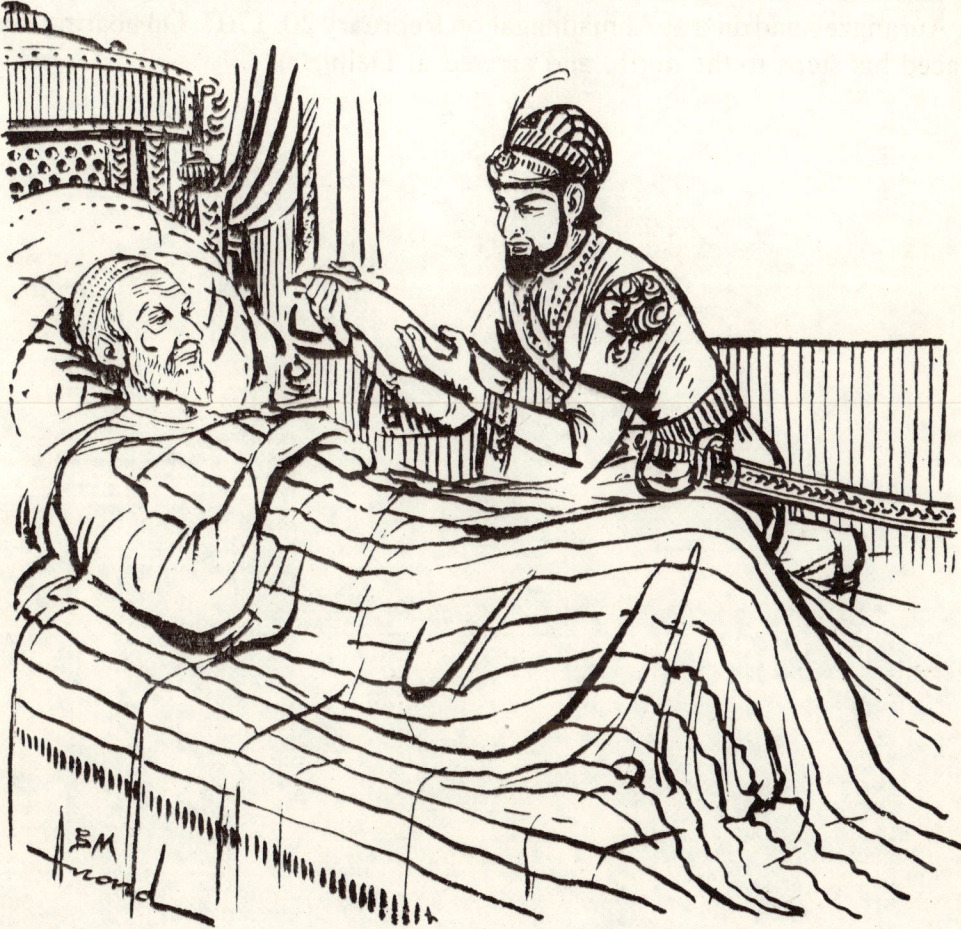

Having learnt from them how difficult and risky it had been for them to travel all the way from Punjab, he gave them a *parwana* (letter) of safe conduct for their return journey.

The Emperor wrote to the Governor of Sarhind, telling him that the Guru should not be troubled or harmed any more. He also issued orders that the Guru should be provided safe conduct and all needed facilities throughout the empire on his way to Ahmadnagar, and if required, be given cash to meet his travelling expenses.

83

On returning to the Guru, Bhai Daya Singh and Dharm Singh conveyed to him Aurangzeb's intense desire to see him. The Guru was deeply moved on learning the Emperor's condition. He decided to accept his invitation, to see him and prepare him for the last journey to appear before his Maker.

So he started towards the Deccan. When he reached near Baghaur, he heard that Aurangzeb had died at Ahmadnagar on February 20, 1707. On hearing this, he retraced his steps to the north, and arrived at Delhi.

MUKTSAR

We have seen that at Dina the Guru was lovingly served by three brothers, named Shamira, Lakhmira and Takht Mal. When the Nawab of Sarhind heard of it, he sent strict orders to the Guru's host Shamira, telling him to arrest the Guru and bring him to Sarhind but Shamira refused to do so.

On receiving Shamira's reply, Wazir Khan, Nawab of Sarhind, decided to march in pursuit of the Guru. Rumours of the Nawab's decision reached Dina. The Guru was prepared to face and fight the Nawab. But he thought, 'If the fight takes place near this or any other village, the inhabitants will be put to much unnecessary trouble.' Hence he decided to move on into the jungle.

He left Dina, accordingly. After passing through a number of villages, he reached Jaito. There he learnt that Nawab Wazir Khan of Sarhind was coming thither with a force of five thousand. He was expected to reach there in four or five days. The Guru decided to move on to near Khidrana. His plan was to face the Mughal army near the lake.

As said already, a few hundred Sikhs deserted the Guru during the siege of Anandpur Sahib. Before leaving, they wrote the 'disclaimer,' putting down in black and white that he was not their Guru and they were not his Sikhs. Forty of the deserters belonged to the Majha tract of Punjab. When they reached their homes, they were rebuked and shamed by their women. The latter did not let them enter their homes. They said, 'Go back to the Guru and make amends for your cowardly conduct. Otherwise, exchange your dress with ours, stay at home, and act as housewives in our place. Dressed in your clothes, we shall go and fight and die for the Guru. In that way we shall wash away with our blood the shame which your conduct has brought on the Sikhs of Majha.'

The deserters accordingly decided to go back. This band of forty fully-armed Saint soldiers started towards the Guru. Mai Bhago of Jhabal also joined them. She and Bhai Mahan Singh of Sursingh were the leaders of that band. They had to travel cautiously. If they marched together, they might be captured. So they travelled in small groups, mostly by night, and by unfrequented, out-of-the-way routes.

The party reached near Khidrana. They learnt that the Guru had shortly before gone over to the other side of the lake. They also learnt that Wazir Khan's army was approaching. It was expected to reach there soon. On reaching Khidrana, they found it was almost dry. Bhai Mahan Singh proposed that the enemy be engaged there. The Guru would, thereby get time to reach some safe place on the other side.

His proposal was accepted. Wide white sheets of cotton were spread on shrubs. They looked like so many tents. The sight of them was sure to make the enemy believe that the Sikhs were encamping there in large numbers.

The Muslim army arrived soon. Long and bloody was the battle which ensued. The Sikhs fought with their usual courage and power. Mai Bhago was fighting in the foremost rank. The Guru had reached a small hill on the other side of Khidrana. From there he directed a constant rain of arrows on the Muslim attackers. A large number of them fell pierced by his arrows. The army made repeated attacks on the Sikhs. Each time it had to go back after suffering heavy losses.

At last the Sikhs' stock of ammunition and arrows was exhausted. They were obliged to have recourse to their swords and spears. They advanced in small groups They engaged the enemy in hand-to-hand fights and killed several times their own members. They went on wielding their weapons most effectively till they were overpowered. They were not fighting for victory. They knew that the enemy was too strong. They have no thought of saving their lives. Their only wish was to check, as long as possible, the enemy's advance against the Guru. In time, all of them lay on the ground. About three thousand Turks lay with them on the same bloody field.

Wazir Khan advanced to take possession of the lake. To his dismay, it was almost dry. It was the month of Baisakh. His army was crying for water. On enquiry he learnt that sufficient water could be had at distance of about fifty kilometres in front and about fifteen kilometres in the rear. He decided to go back and save his army from dying of thirst.

After the Muslim army had gone, the Guru visited the scene of the battle. Among the Sikhs who had died fighting he found those forty men of Majha who had deserted his ranks during the siege of Anandpur Sahib, but who, shamed by their women who would not let them enter their homes, had come back to reinforce his small army. With fatherly affection he lifted the heads of the martyrs into his lap, one by one, wiped their faces and blessed them. In due time it was Bhai Mahan Singh's turn to be thus caressed and blessed. The Guru found that still there was some life in him. After a time he opened his eyes. He found himself in the Guru's lap and arms. He was filled with immense joy. The Guru asked him if he had any wish to be fulfilled. 'No father,' replied Bhai Mahan Singh. 'I have seen you. I die for your cause, in your lap, and with your blessings. What else or more could I desire? But father, if you have taken compassion on us here, tear off our 'disclaimer', the paper on which we wrote, 'You are not our Guru, we are not your Sikhs.' Tear it off, forgive us, take us all back in your fold, and let the broken ties be re-united.'

The Guru was highly pleased to hear Bhai Mahan Singh's last wish. He blessed him and said, 'You have done a great deed. You have saved the root of Sikhism in Majha. You and your companions, all forty of you, are *muktas*—the Saved Ones. This battle field shall be called Muktsar or the Pool of Salvation. You are delivered from the chain of births and deaths for ever. You have attained *mukti*, freedom from birth and death.' The forty *muktas* are, and shall ever be, remembered in the Sikh prayer.

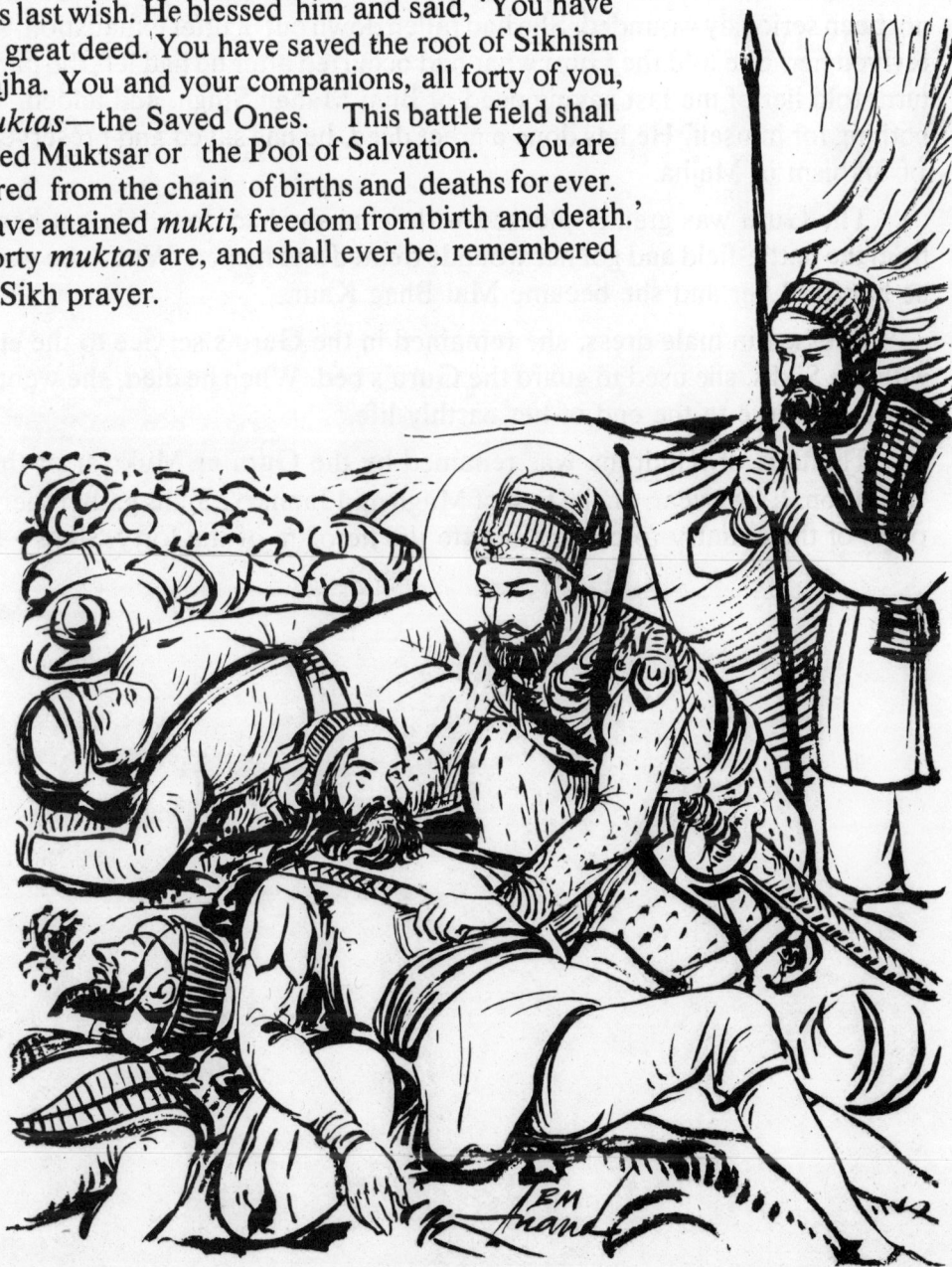

The Guru then took out the disclaimer from under his belt, tore it into tiny pieces, and threw it away. Bhai Mahan Singh saw this. He felt immensely relieved. He smiled, took a long, deep breath, and closed his eyes for ever.

Then the Guru went to the place where Mai Bhago was lying senseless. She had not been seriously wounded. She had fallen down out of utter exhaustion. A little aid revived her. She told the Guru what had occurred after he had left the party. He, in turn, told her of the last saving deed of Bhai Mahan Singh, and added, 'He asked nothing for himself. He has done a great deed, he has saved and preserved the root of Sikhism in Majha.'

The Guru was greatly pleased with what she had done. He got her removed from the battle-field and got her wounds treated and healed. When she was all right, he baptized her and she became Mai Bhag Kaur.

Dressed in male dress, she remained in the Guru's service to the end. Along with ten Sikhs, she used to guard the Guru's bed. When he died, she went to Bidar, and lived there to the end of her earthly life.

The tank of Khidrana was renamed by the Guru as Muktsar or the Pool of Salvation. Every year, on the first of Magh mid January, Sikhs gather there from all parts of the country to commemorate the heroism of the forty Sikhs—*muktas*.

SOUTHWARD HO!

The Guru continued his onward journey. In all places visited by him he urged the people to follow the principles of Sikh religion, and lead lives of love, service, and devotion, to earn their living by honest labour, and to share their earnings with the poor and the needy. In all places large numbers were baptized and made members of the Khalsa Brotherhood.

It has to be remembered that the Guru had engaged a large number of Malwa Sikhs, mostly Brars, as paid soldiers. For some time it had not been possible to pay them regularly. Again and again they pressed him to clear their accounts and let them go. He advised them to wait a little longer, assuring them that all their claims would be duly settled. But they grew impatient. One day they held up his horse by the reins and refused to let him proceed until they were paid. 'Wait a little longer', said the Guru to them. 'God will send sufficient money to meet your claims. You know the risks that I am in just now. Let us proceed to a safer place.'

But those Brar Sikhs of Malwa had no regard for the risks which he was talking of. So they said, 'No, we have waited too long already. We refuse to wait a minute longer. From here we will not move, nor let you move, till all our dues are paid. If you need us further in your service, promise to double our pay.'

The Guru smiled and said, 'Well, make your choice. Choose between me and the object of your greed. Will you have the Sikh faith or silver coins?'

'Sikhs we already are,' replied the Malwa Brars. 'The Sikh faith we already have. Give us silver. We desire nothing else.'

Just then a Sikh arrived with a large load of gold and silver coins. They were heaped on the ground at the Guru's bidding. He then told the Brars to come, one by one, and get their arrears of pay. In this way they were all paid what was due to them. Then the Guru asked their leader, Dana, at what rate he should be paid. Dana begged the Guru to allow him to remain with him as his Sikh. This reply pleased the Guru, 'Well done, Dana dear,' said he, 'You have preserved the foundation of the faith in Malwa, as Mahan Singh and his companions did in Mahja. Now take the *amrit* and become a Khalsa.'

Dana became Dana Singh. At his loving invitation, the Guru changed his course towards the village of this faithful saint-soldier. At some distance from the village, there was a beautiful green forest which stretched as far as and beyond the horizon. The Guru decided to halt there. He was charmed by the natural scenery of the place. He called it the Lakhi jungle and decided to stay there for some time.

Disciples from far and near came in large numbers to see their long-separated Master. Anandpur was reproduced there in all its joys and blessings. Hundreds were baptized and made members of the Khalsa Panth. Among those who were thus baptized there was a Muslim *faqir* named Ibrahim. After baptism he became Ajmer Singh. He was the first Muslim to be baptized. He accompanied the Guru in his further journey.

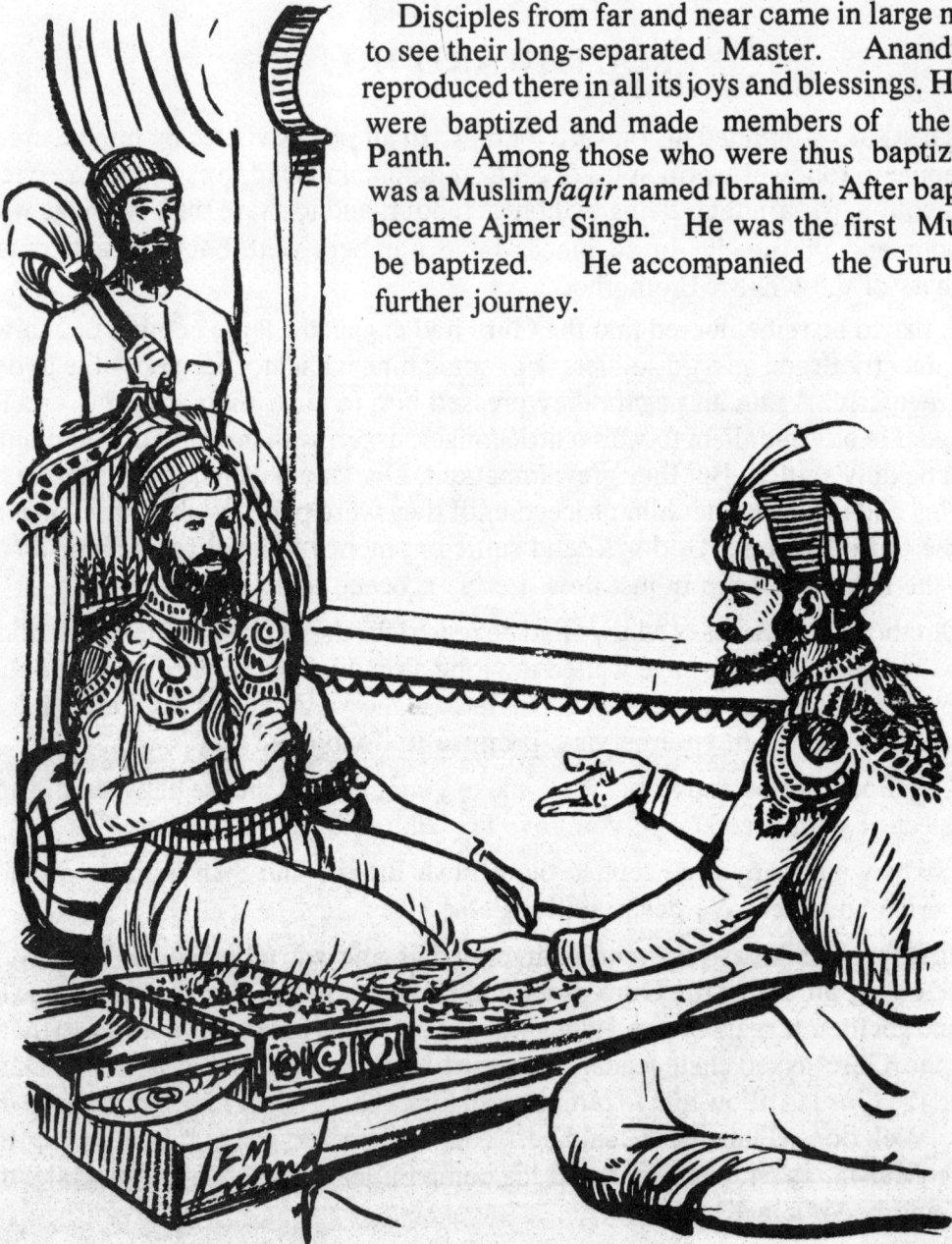

Leaving the Lakhi jungle, and passing through many villages, the Guru reached Talwandi Sabo, now called Damdama Sahib or the Sacred Resting Place. He stayed there for about nine months with an influential Sikh named Dalla, who after baptism became Dalla Singh. He made the place a seat of learning. It is often described as the Guru's Kashi. While at Damdama Sahib, the Guru re-edited the Holy Granth and gave it the final form which became fixed for all time.

After about nine months' stay at Damdama Sahib, the Guru resumed his journy to the Deccan. When he reached the neighbourhood of Baghaur he heard the news that Aurangzeb had died in his camp at Ahmadnagar. Thereupon the Guru returned to Delhi.

Aurangzeb's sons began to fight for the throne. Bahadur Shah, who was the eldest, requested the Guru for help in this war of succession. The Guru hepled him with a detachment of his selected soldiers under the command of Bhai Dharam Singh. On June 8, 1707 a battle was fought at Jajau near Agra, where Bahadur Shah was victorious. He became the Emperor. He invited the Guru to Agra, where he received him with great honour. He presented him with a rich dress of honour and a jewelled scarf *(dhukhdhuki)* worth sixty thousand rupees. The Guru was pleased with the interview, and saw in it the possiblity of ending the age-old differences with the Mughals.

While the negotiations were still in progress, Bahadur Shah had to march to Rajasthan and thence to the Deccan. He requested the Guru to accompany him. The Guru accompanied him for a long time. At every place of halt, he separated himself from the royal camp to preach his mission to the people. After a time, the Guru saw that there was no prospect of the Emperor's agreeing to any proposal for the redress of his wrongs. He broke off with the Emperor and came to Nander in the beginning of September, 1707.

RETURN TO THE ETERNAL HOME

At Nander in the Deccan, there was, near the bank of the river Godavari, the *ashram* or resting place of Bairagi monk named Madho Das. The Bairagi possessed great magical powers. With their help he used to play practical jokes on those who came to see him.

When the Guru arrived at the *ashram*, Madho Das was away. The Guru went in and occupied the Bairagi's couch. He told his Sikhs to kill one of the Bairagi's goats and cook it for dinner. One of the Bairagi's disciples ran to inform him of the visitor and his conduct. The Bairagi flew into a fit of rage. With his magical power he tried to overturn the couch occupied by the Guru. But he failed. He had never failed before. He was astonished and upset. He went to the *ashram*. There he made another effort at magic. But he failed again. He was convinced that the visitor had far greater powers than he. He went before the Guru. The following dialogue took place between them.

Madho Das : Who are you ?

Guru Gobind Singh : He whom you know.

Madho Das : What do I know ?

Guru Gobind Singh : Think it over.

Madho Das : (after a short pause) So you are Guru Gobind Singh.

Guru Gobind Singh : Yes.

Madho Das : What have you come here for ?

Guru Gobind Singh : I have come to make you my disciple.

Madho Das : I submit. I am your Banda (slave).

Saying this, he fell at the Guru's feet. The Guru instructed him in the tenets of the Sikh faith. In due course he baptized him. On taking the *amrit*, Madho Das became Banda Singh. In Sikh history he is popularly known as Banda Bahadur or Banda Singh Bahadur. After a time the Guru sent him to Punjab as the leader of the Khalsa.

Now, Wazir Khan the Nawab of Sarhind, was still an enemy of the Guru. He had been as we know, responsible for most of the Guru's sufferings. He became alarmed to learn that the Guru's relations with Bahadur Shah were growing closer

and closer, day by day. He knew what would happen to him if peace were made between the Emperor and the Sikhs. It was believed that the Guru had a special object in accompanying the Emperor. That object was to get Wazir Khan, murderer of the Guru's sons, duly punished. Already the Emperor had shown an inclination to help the Guru at Wazir Khan's expense. He had granted a *firman* (order) in favour of the Guru, ordering Wazir Khan to pay the Guru three hundred rupees a day. Wazir Khan was, therefore, in fear of his life. He feared that the Guru might prevail upon the Emperor to punish him for his cruel, murderous acts. He could not feel safe or secure as long as the Guru was alive. He, therefore, planned to get the Guru murdered.

He hired two young Pathans and deputed them to murder the Guru. They pursued the latter secretly on his journey to the South. They came to Nander. They paid occasional visits to the Guru. In this way they became acquainted with the Guru and his attendant Sikhs. One day after the evening service, one of them went near the bed on which the Guru was taking rest. The Guru gave him *parshad* (some sweets), which he devoured at once. Then he took his seat near the Guru's bed. After a time the Guru felt sleepy. He closed his eyes. His sole attendant also happened to be sleepy. The Pathan saw his chance. He sprang to his feet, drew his sword, and stabbed the Guru. Before he could deal another blow, he was cut down by the Guru with his sword. Then he called out to his Sikhs. Many came up running. The Pathan's companion tried to escape, but he fell under the swords of the Sikhs who had come on hearing the noise and the Guru's call.

The Guru's wound was immediately sewn up. In a few days it appeared to have healed up. But one day he tried to bend a stiff bow which a Sikh had presented to him. His imperfectly healed wound burst open. It began to bleed profusely. The Guru felt that the end of his earthly life was near. He had already conferred the guruship on the Khalsa at Chamkaur Sahib. That was about secular affairs. He had then said that there was to be no personal Guru after him: no man was to be regarded as the Guru. Regarding matters religious and spiritual, he now formally conferred the guruship on the Holy Granth. Having placed five paise and a coconut before the Sacred Granth, he went round it thrice and then bowed before it.

Then he gave his parting message to his Sikhs. He said. 'The system of personal Guru ends with me. There will be no eleventh or twelfth Guru of the Sikhs. Such are the orders of the Almighty Father. The Khalsa Panth will guide itself by the teachings of the Guru as incorporated in Guru Granth Sahib. Whenever you need my advice or guidance, gather in the presence of Guru Granth Sahib, and disucss and decide things in the light of the Gurus' teachings embodied therein. Whenever a group of my Sikhs remembers and calls upon me with true hearts and pure minds, I shall ever be in their midst. Love the Word, the Sacred Gurbani, love and serve the Panth. Preserve the Khalsa uniform, the Khalsa identity, and the Khalsa principles.

Then he lay down and returned to the Eternal Home from where he had come. This happened on October 7, 1708 A.D. He was then less than forty two years of age.

94